U.S. OCCUPATION IN EUROPE AFTER WORLD WAR II

**A George C. Marshall
Research Foundation Publication**

U.S. OCCUPATION IN EUROPE AFTER WORLD WAR II

Papers and Reminiscences from
the April 23-24, 1976, Conference
Held at the George C. Marshall
Research Foundation,
Lexington, Virginia

Edited with an Introduction
by

Hans A. Schmitt

The Regents Press of Kansas
Lawrence

Library of Congress Cataloging in Publication Data
Main entry under title:

U.S. occupation in Europe after World War II.

"A George C. Marshall Research Foundation publication."
Includes bibliographical references and index.

1. Germany—History—Allied occupation, 1945–
—Congresses. 2. Germany, West—Politics and government
—Congresses. 3. Austria—History—Allied occupation,
1945–1955—Congresses. 4. Clay, Lucius DuBignon,
1897–   —Congresses. I. Schmitt, Hans A.

II. George C. Marshall Research Foundation.

DD257.U54   355.4′9   78-51611

ISBN 0-7006-0178-3
ISBN 0-7006-0179-3 pbk.

Table of Contents

Preface

A word about the origin of this volume may help the reader put it in its proper perspective.

In 1976—thirty years after the Allied Occupation Powers were in the midst of their activities in Germany and Austria—the George C. Marshall Research Foundation convened a conference to consider United States Occupation policy from the vantage point of three decades after its implementation.

In addition to the opportunity for this historical retrospective, the conference was unique in its participants. On the one hand, six scholars of the period provided papers on significant aspects of the occupation of Germany and Austria. They were: John W. Atwell, Hollins College; Barbara Ann Chotiner, now Library of Congress; Milton Colvin, Washington and Lee University; John Gimbel, Humboldt State University; Jean E. Smith, University of Toronto, and Earl Ziemke, University of Georgia. At the same time, nine senior officials of the American government who were personally involved in these policies took part in the conference discussion and a special roundtable on the subject. They were: Ambassador Jacob D. Beam, Ambassador Ernest A. Gross, Governor W. Averell Harriman, The Honorable John J. McCloy, Ambassador Robert D. Murphy, The Honorable Paul H. Nitze, The Honorable Jacque J. Reinstein, and Ambassador James W. Riddleberger. It was my privilege also to be associated with these men in both the War and State Departments. Finally a group of discussants from both government and academic life added their judgments to the conference. They were: William M. Franklin, formerly of the State Department, Whittle Johnston, the University of Virginia, Barry F. Machado, Washington and Lee University, Bernard F. Morris, the University of Indiana; Forrest C. Pogue, the biographer of General Marshall; George K. Romoser, University of New Hampshire; and Donald R. Whitnah, University of Northern Iowa.

Two key personalities of the period, General Lucius D. Clay, U.S. Military Governor for Germany, and General Mark W. Clark, U.S. High Commissioner for Austria, were prevented at the last minute from attending the conference because of health reasons. However, both were interviewed at length, and their reflections were summarized by the Director of the Marshall Foundation, Fred L. Hadsel, while highlights of the views of the principal policy participants were prepared by Charles W. Sydnor, Longwood College. The entire volume has been edited by Hans A. Schmitt, the University of Virginia, who has written the introduction as well.

This book is the distillation of a unique conference. It is the belief of all concerned that the composition of the conference together with the high quality of the papers added significantly to the value of this volume for students and scholars of this formative post-war period of history.

Charles E. Saltzman
Conference Chairman

U.S. OCCUPATION IN EUROPE AFTER WORLD WAR II

1

Introduction

1806, 1918, 1945:

Three German Catastrophes

Hans A. Schmitt
The University of Virginia

Throughout medieval and modern times, Germany and Austria have shared the same political jurisdiction. Their association ended in 1866 but was briefly restored in 1938. Seven years later, total military defeat forced a second separation.

The final catastrophe and its immediate political consequences were the subject of a symposium held at the George C. Marshall Research Foundation in Lexington, Virginia on April 23–24, 1976. The meeting brought together prominent American policy-makers and scholars. For the better part of two days, the architects and chroniclers of history reviewed what had happened and why. Scholars' papers and a summary of the reflections of the history-makers characterized the essence of these deliberations and constitute the bulk of this volume. The following introduction tries to explain as succinctly as possible how Germany and Austria came to this turning point.

I

The modern history of the German-speaking world divides into two different and unequal parts. One, from the fourteenth to the end of the eighteenth century, represents a time in which secular institutions changed little; the other, extending from the threshold of the nineteenth century to the present, represents an epoch in which no settlement outlasted an average lifetime. The first ended amidst calls for revolution; the second produced a growing hunger for stability.

The largest part of this semi-millenium unfolded in the shadow of the Holy Roman Empire's awe-inspiring continuity, dominated since 1452 by the Habsburg dynasty. In the late seventeenth and early eighteenth centuries, some of the most powerful vassals of the emperor made large conquests outside the empire and joined the ranks of Europe's sovereign ruler.[1] The transformations enfeebled imperial authority by introducing absolutist government at the second level of the empire's political structure.

The Holy Roman Empire survived these anomalies until it was destroyed by Napoleon Bonaparte in 1806. Polycentric and unintegrated, the empire's involved history left Germans with a sense of inferiority for lacking the discipline and vigor which welded Englishmen, Frenchmen, and Spaniards into strong political states. Their frustration was compounded by the fact that a French leader at the head of French armies, rather than a domestic revolution, put an end to this hoary framework of German disunity.

Napoleon's success did not indicate, of course, that the Holy Roman Empire could no longer function but merely that it lacked the strength to defend itself against the national energies mobilized in revolutionary France. Napoleon's victory tells us very little about the quality of the German past, but what remains important to us is the German response to the Corsican invader. That response revealed a pliable, docile people capable of accepting whatever fate imposed. Germans allowed Napoleon to use them and their resources for his own ends. They let him rearrange, reconstruct, and exploit as he saw fit. Rebellion against his tyranny was rare. At most, one can say that instances of German resistance were more than balanced by instances of unquestioning devotion to the French empire, as manifested in 1814 by the Westphalian garrison of Küstrin which held the fortress on the Oder until ten days before the capitulation of Paris.[2]

As a result, Bonaparte designed the first European polity whose population spoke only German, the Confederation of the Rhine. In a

4

INTRODUCTION

minimal sense, the Confederation served as a model for all future German states. Moreover, all German solutions after 1815 stemmed from French experiments and experience. Prussian military reforms were conceived and executed by officers who often carried the books of Jean Jacques Rousseau in their knapsacks. Many German veterans of the wars against Napoleon, no matter how they hated France, sought to plant on German soil the institutions of the French Revolution. Even after that revolution had been followed by restoration at home, France's new fundamental law—the Charter of 1814—served as a model for the first German constitutional experiments of the nineteenth century. The radical solutions adopted by the Revolution of 1848 included a national parliament elected by universal manhood suffrage as well as a bill of rights inspired by the 1791 Declaration of the Rights of Man and the Citizen.[3]

Liberty, equality, and brotherhood were not all that Napoleon bequeathed to future German generations. His destruction of the empire also freed a number of German princes from their allegiance to the emperor. The new age attired the princes with sovereignty and enabled them to introduce, belatedly, the precepts of absolute monarchy. The new kings and granddukes pitted the divisive powers of dynastic particularism against the unifying impulses emanating from the revolutionary doctrines of national loyalty. In 1848 their parochial interest, organized since 1815 in a confederation reaching from Hamburg to Vienna and from the Baltic Sea to the Black Forest, crushed national democratic aspirations. Dominated by monarchical strength and the privilege of inheritance, the princes preserved the retrograde aspects of Napoleonic influence.

Liberal and democratic failure[4] was due most obviously to the weakness of the democratic movement, the weakness of national sentiment, and the revolution's lack of experienced, vigorous leadership. Finally, the constellation of fatal defects was supplemented by a surprising inability to decide just what a German national movement should unify.

In Europe, unlike the Americas and Africa, the most important characteristic of national identity has been language. In the case of Germany, however, the opportunity to fashion a nation-state extending "as far as sounds the German tongue" vanished centuries ago, when the Peace of Westphalia (1648) granted independence to the Dutch and the Swiss. At the same time, the most powerful German dynasties had expanded deep into Eastern and Southeastern Europe. The distillation of a nation from this growing complex of dynastically and ethnically divided territories became increasingly difficult. The king of Prussia ruled over millions of Poles. The Austrian emperor was also king of Hungary and of

Bohemia and ruled not only Magyars and Czechs, but Slovaks, Croats, Slovenes, and Rumanians. How could a Germanic Confederation, of which these two sovereigns had, since 1815, been the dominant members, be transformed into a national polity? Whatever else the Revolution of 1848 may have failed to achieve, it reduced the possibilities to two: a future German state which would include Austria—though not its foreign subjects—and become "Greater Germany," or a state which would exclude Austria, be led by Prussia, and represent a "Little Germany."

Until a decision had been reached between these two choices, the German world remained unstable and disunited. Nationalists opposed particularists, democrats opposed liberals, and liberals opposed both democrats on the left and conservatives on the right. At the same time, nationalists divided between supporters of Austria and partisans of Prussia. Some particularists would accept a Greater Germany under the first, while rejecting the Little Germany solution under the second. Finally, there remained the dilemma facing many liberals: could they prefer unity over liberty without betraying their principles?

The eventual solution to this dilemma reflected the pragmatic character of its creator, Bismarck. The short-lived German national state which existed between 1871 and 1945 embodied both conservative and democratic principles. It reflected a founder who was Prussian and whose upbringing had been conservative, hence its Little German scope and the maximal preservation of particularist and dynastic institutions.

During Bismarck's early years in public office, the national state appropriated a remarkable dependence on armed might and a predilection for democratic ritual from the Bonapartist revival in France. Subsequent generations were to assign paramount importance to the military rather than the democratic aspects of unification. This led to a dangerously simplified view of the nature of the German state. For the next 70 years, the entire world mistook the Prussian victories of the 1860s as the achievement of a traditionally militaristic state, forgetting that Prussia had never been a German Sparta.[5] The territorial growth between 1640 and 1795, which turned Prussia into the largest German state after Austria, was not a result of military conquest but mainly a product of felicitous marriages and crafty dynastic diplomacy. Even that brilliant royal captain, Frederick the Great (1712–1786), gained more land through negotiation than through war. Except for Frederick's reign, Prussia's military record presented an ordinary blend in which failures outnumbered successes. The defeat of Bonaparte in 1815 owed infinitely more to British stubbornness and Russian capacity for suffering than to Prussian skill at arms. Bismarck's single-minded and extralegal pursuit of

6

military reform in 1862 itself indicates that once again the Hohenzollern military machine had lost whatever eminence it might have occasionally possessed in the past. Both the victories over Austria in 1866 and over France in 1871 surprised all Europe which, basing its estimates on past experience, had expected Prussia to be defeated in both encounters. Only after the second Bonaparte emperor had, on September 2, 1870, surrendered his sword to William I of Prussia, did the world and the Germans themselves begin to see the Prussian kingdom and, subsequently, the German nation, as exponents of unparalleled military discipline and know-how. Only then was the myth born of German "militarism" which in time hypnotized the Germans quite as much as it did their enemies.

Lately, historians have begun to appreciate that the support of a large industrial complex, which had been expanding rapidly since the 1820s, played an equally indispensable part in Germany's unification.[6] The German settlement of 1815 had added the Saar, the Ruhr, and the Siegerland, with their treasures of coal and iron ore, to Prussia's natural resources in Silesia. The postwar kingdom, stretching from the heart of Poland to the eastern boundary of France, had initiated a new economic order by abolishing guild privileges and internal tariff barriers, followed by a succession of bilateral agreements with other German states which expanded the Prussian customs union into a German one. By excluding Austria from this "common market," Prussia confirmed its economic hegemony over Germany well before the military showdown of 1866 added the requisite dimensions of military and political control.

The masters of the resulting wealth in banking and commerce obviously occupied their own strategic heights on the road to Prussia's conquest of the German fatherland. They were not Prussian *Junker*, dedicated to serving the Hohenzollern dynasty, but represented a new estate recruited from diverse backgrounds, rarely nobles, often sons of civil servants, physicians, teachers and clergymen.[7] Although many at first opposed what they mistook as Bismarck's single-minded pursuit of military expansion at the expense of parliament and constitution, they were soon relieved to find that the iron Chancellor's victories did not affect Prussia's role as the German haven of laissez-faire. After the new army defeated Denmark in 1864, the acquisition of Kiel, with its splendid harbor, spoke the unequivocal language of commercial expansion. Two years later Prussian annexation of Hanover facilitated the shipment of Prussian coal to the major markets of Hamburg and Bremen.

Preservation of dynasties, maximization of military might, and economic expansion, while playing to the gallery of free enterprise, played key roles in creating the nation-state. The final ingredient, a veneer of democracy, perfected the edifice. Although the Germanic Confederation had ignored Bismarck's call for a parliament in the spring of 1866, and although parliamentary advocates never quite trusted the Prussian leader's espousal of their cause, Germany's founding father created a parliament as a major constitutional feature of his new empire. In a sense, the parliament was designed to hold together the entire monument, joining the liberal entrepreneur to a conservative national monarchy. The parliament was chosen by universal manhood suffrage, and Bismarck expected it to be equally conservative. He reasoned that the voters, economically and psychologically dependent on rural landlords or industrial employers, would exercise their franchise in favor of the established order. He counted on the common man to contain the liberal elite.

II

The German empire, accordingly, turned out to be a hybrid creature, although to all appearances a healthy one. No other emerging modern nation was born as sturdy. No other new nation began its history as an uncontested great power. No new polity would ever again possess the military resources to assure its own security and, so promptly upon emergence, declare itself "saturated." From the moment of its founding, Germany could function as a stabilizer and pacifier in international affairs.

But even in unity, the Germans remained troubled. Recent post-mortems of Bismarck's achievement point to the massive emotional letdown following unification.[8] For the generation which had achieved sovereign statehood for the nation, victory also meant lost purpose.

Added to the resulting malaise were the problems which national victory either produced or failed to resolve. Among these was the fear of losing what had just been gained. To be sure, France remained the major foreign opponent of nationhood, and she had been defeated and occupied. But unification also coincided with the end of the First Vatican Council. This unprecedented conclave proclaimed the doctrine of Papal Infallibility on July 13, 1870. To many Germans this new written affirmation of authority on behalf of Pius IX, the author of the Syllabus of Errors which had castigated liberalism, nationalism and democracy, appeared to be a deliberate clerical challenge to their new national state. Liberals and Protestants feared that it would threaten the national loyalties of their Catholic fellow citizens. They anticipated, furthermore, that when secular governments erred in the future, Rome would assume the position of *arbiter mundi*. Because of its domestic impact, this threat

8

from a foreign power without an army became important. As the new government in Berlin surveyed its expanded jurisdiction, it found reason to dread the possible clash between civilizations (*Kulturkampf*) which papal pretensions portended. Germany's Polish minority of 3½ million and the 1½ million men and women inhabiting the newly conquered province of Alsace-Lorraine constituted a significant portion of the 20 million Roman Catholics in Germany. Their loyalties were uncertain. Nor could Bismarck forget the majority "Patriot Party" which had opposed German unification on the floor of the Bavarian parliament until three days after the proclamation of the empire. Much of the Patriot Party's leadership came from the priesthood, while its rank and file was overwhelmingly Catholic. Thus, at the moment of supreme German triumph, the Roman Church emerged as the suspected focus of a disloyal opposition.

In time, it turned out, of course, that German Catholics were as loyal as their Protestant fellow citizens. Still, the campaign against them died only after a new threat appeared on the horizon: Socialism.

The second wave of national hysteria deriving from Socialism was the product of the Depression of 1873, when bankruptcies and unemployment provided a sufficient cause for an early decline of patriotic exaltation. A new uncertainty gripped the country driving the affluent into the arms of conservatism, splintering and decimating the liberal ranks, and persuading the lower classes to listen to the "siren song of Socialism," as Bismarck put it. The Chancellor's confidence in the inherent conservatism of the masses was shaken. Two attempts on the life of the beloved patriarch William I heightened tensions and provided the pretext for a bill outlawing the Socialist Party. For the first and last time before the advent of Hitler, a political group representing a significant portion of the people suffered proscription in time of peace. But in an age which had not yet developed persecution into a science, the measure was not effective. Even complementary legislation between 1883 and 1887 which endowed Germany with the most advanced social legislation of the age could not convert the Socialist constituency to Bismarckian national conservatism. The movement disappeared in name only, and by the turn of the century, after the ineffectual edict of suppression had been repealed, it turned out to have more members than any other political sect in the Reich.

By that time, William I (1797–1888) had died, and Bismarck had been forced into retirement. A new Kaiser had succeeded, one confident that he could take the place of both founding fathers, fill the dual role of sovereign and head of government, and lead his nation into a new era of greatness.

William II (1857–1941) possessed enthusiasm and ambition, but he lacked political talent or insight. For this reason, he damaged Germany both when he succeeded and when he failed. He transformed the emperor from a remote father figure into a popular national leader.[9] At the same time, he reduced the Imperial Chancellor, whose office had been designed for and identified with the baronial majesty of a Bismarck, into a well-paid bureaucrat, wholly dependent on the favor and caprice of the monarch.

Both changes increased the monarchy's scope and significance. Had William II grown along with his duties, he would have lived to occupy a distinguished place among history's heroes. But nothing in his thirty-year reign succeeded. The fundamental cause of his failures was an inability to understand that solemn pronouncements from the throne did not, by themselves, constitute policies. As a result, his reign remains largely a record of verbal excesses and political inactivity. When aroused, William would vow to smash those that opposed him, make a blood-bath of Socialists, or hang recalcitrant opponents in parliament. His subjects from the Chancellor on down soon learned, however, that barking Hohenzollerns did not bite.

Political opposition grew, and crucial government bills suffered igno-minious defeat. The last national election under the empire in 1912 crowned a succession of domestic failures. Of 397 parliamentary mandates, 110 went to the Socialists. Of Germany's 12.5 million voters, 7.5 million opted for opposition parties.[10]

The emergence of a self-styled revolutionary and republican party as the largest single political organization in the land also owed much to the country's growth as an industrial nation. Few leaders in government, from the Kaiser on down, knew how to cope with this transformation. Storms of social change drowned out their impotent appeals to traditional loyalties. The most powerful single element in social democracy was the growing labor union movement which organized heavy industry, notably miners, metal and textile workers. As these trades became increasingly indispensable underpinnings of national wealth, they achieved an un-precedented freedom of action through organization. As early as 1897, the German parliament defeated a government measure threatening advocates of industrial strikes with heavy jail sentences. In the first decade of the new century, textile workers and miners turned the strike into an effective weapon in their successful quest for higher wages and better working conditions.

The Socalists' large concentration of republican voters also reflected the declining vigor of monarchy. If Bismarck had misjudged the future voting behavior of the masses, his unique compromise between tradition and revolution had likewise not worked well. His system enabled 25 sovereign princes to survive unification but left only one of them, the king of Prussia, who became emperor, with a sovereign function. The others led empty ceremonial lives, sometimes tarnished by scandal. Mad Ludwig's extravagant construction projects threatened Bavarian finances and led to his forcible removal from the throne in 1886. King Karl I of Württemberg's succession of male lovers, some of whom he rewarded with titles of nobility, were about to provoke a similar coup d'état when a convenient heart attack ended his reign. In 1903 the Crown Princess of Saxony deserted her husband and five children for a life of international adventure, crowned by the publication of her memoirs in German, English, French, and Italian. These were only the peaks in a proliferating *chronique scandaleuse* revealing the demi-gods of German dynasticism to be idlers, fornicators, and madmen.

William's inability to prevent, cover up, or redress these failings constituted another measure of his ineptness as chief of state. The other German princes accorded him the ceremonial respect due his position but never asked his advice. When it was offered, they made a point of publicly disregarding it.

Abroad, unfortunately, the Kaiser's pronouncements were taken far more seriously than at home, and William II's purely verbal ferocity contributed to his empire's gradual isolation in international affairs. A contemporary reviewer observed in 1907 that his speeches sounded "as if all of Germany continuously rattled down the street with sabres drawn."[11] Bismarck's strong, saturated empire, a state cultivating the low profile, had been replaced by a more problematic, insecure land, led by men who sought to hide their weakness behind an unceasing cannonade of martial speeches.

The ability to antagonize strangers also poisoned relations with the empire's ethnic and cultural minorities long after the *Kulturkampf* had become a chapter in history textbooks. Germany held its Poles in contempt, even as it feared their high birthrate and subjected them to various ill-conceived economic and cultural Germanization policies, all of which ended in failure. As the Polish population grew in number, its alienation from the state increased. The government also subjected the 140,000 Danes in North Schleswig to intensive and fruitless cultural pressures, earning their lasting disaffection.[12]

Most humiliating in the long run, however, was the empire's failure to convert the German-speaking majority of Alsace-Lorraine into loyal subjects of the house of Hohenzollern. Because of its strategic position on the border with France, Alsace-Lorraine was denied self-government and organized instead as an "imperial territory" (*Reichsland*). A civilian viceroy and a general officer commanding the large garrisons in Metz and Strasbourg functioned as duel proconsuls. In 1911, Germany finally granted Alsace-Lorraine the equivalent of a state constitution, but it came too late to dissipate local antagonism. In 1913, the historian Hans Delbrück confessed that the inhabitants of the *Reichsland* still "refused to belong to the German people."[13] Early in December 1914, the writer Ernst Toller, stationed in Alsace, was told by his commanding officer that "the place was alive with suspicious persons . . . against whose machinations we must guard ourselves" to the point of locking doors "and sleeping with our weapons beside us."[14]

The failure to win the hearts and minds of a population whose acquisition from France in 1871 had been celebrated as liberation rather than conquest prompted the 1913 session of the Reichstag to pass overwhelmingly (293 to 55) the first resolution of government censure in its history. The unprecedented protest, however, signalled no upsurge of parliamentary power in national affairs. Vigor and determination never thrived on the benches of the imperial *Reichstag*. The vote on Alsace-Lorraine, as it turned out, relieved the collective conscience of its liberal and Socialist majority. The issue was then dropped, and this demonstration, too, remained verbal, illustrating that irresponsible and empty oratory had become a disease infecting the entire nation. Since parliament showed no sign of issuing a sustained challenge, Kaiser and bureaucracy remained the masters of Germany. The empire failed to negotiate a transition to meaningful constitutional monarchy, because parliament did not support such a change. Conservatives, Catholic Centrists, and National Liberals preferred the status quo. Progressives spoke for a strong parliament but feared the Socialists more than their inept sovereign.

After enumerating some of the countless errors and failures of Wilhelmian government, one is bound to be nonplussed to find that, until 1917, no German seriously advocated the overthrow of the empire. People complained, and they criticized. A growing repertory of derisive jokes developed about the Kaiser,[15] but his subjects' steadfastness was not shaken, even when their garrulous commander in chief sat idly by as his bumbling advisers, military and civilian, involved the country in a bloody, prolonged, and disastrous war. Whether Conservative or Socialist, whether German, Pole, Dane or Alsatian, whether Protestant, Catholic or Jew, every subject responded dutifully to universal mobilization. The following recollection by a Socialist member of parliament illustrates one phase of such loyalty:

... on August 3 ... I travelled from Dortmund to Berlin to attend the Party meeting ... at which the question of voting the war credits was to be decided. ... I shall never forget the crowded incidents of those days. I saw reservists join the columns and go forth singing Social Democrat songs! ... Just before the train started ... a group of reservists ... said to me: ". . . you're going to Berlin, to the Reichstag. Think of us there. See to it that we have all we need. Don't be stingy in voting money."[16]

To be sure, each year of war left new fissures in the edifice of unity. Discontent grew with each cut in the food ration and with the passing of each offensive that began as prelude to victory and ended in stalemate. But no matter how bitter the disappointments and how long the casualty lists, a stoic nation suffered on. No German Robespierre, no German Lenin called the people to the barricades. Even the Socialists urged German workers to defend a society which offered them a living standard unequalled in the remainder of Europe. Pressed by defeat in the last weeks of the war, the Kaiser accepted a great retreat on the home front— more drastic even than the simultaneous retreat in the field—when he accepted a constitutional amendment which made the government responsible to parliament. His critics have claimed that he offered too little, too late. But this is true only because the Allies refused to make peace with him, not because Germans athirst for democracy had finally decided to send him packing. In 1918 as in 1806, foreign powers forced Germany to change its government.

III

The year 1918 was, of course, a bad year for reconstitutive reflection. After a war which the country had, from the start, lacked the resources to see through, the nation was physically and emotionally exhausted. To its crushing burdens were added the jolt of a totally unanticipated defeat, the Kaiser's flight to Holland, and the conditions of abject surrender attending the armistice.

Every facet of the catastrophe found Germans equally unprepared. How could their armies win battle after battle and then lose the war? How could a Hohenzollern desert? What had brought the empire to a point where it could not even *negotiate* a peace? The average citizen possessed no answers to these questions. He was therefore ready to accept any explanation which poured balm on his battered psyche. Friedrich Ebert, a saddler who had risen through the ranks of the labor movement to the chairmanship of the Socialist Party, became head of the government in November 1918. When he greeted the first returning contingents of Germany's thoroughly beaten army with the consoling news that they remained "undefeated on the field of battle," he initiated the process of national therapy. Everybody, including the imperial generals and ministers who knew better, agreed to support a myth needed to sustain national self-respect: the game had obviously been lost, but not because Germany was genuinely beaten, but because someone, somewhere, must have cheated.

Germany was experiencing the self-serving reaction of a nation in shock—a nation incapable of rational, purposeful reflection and incapable of constructive policy formation either on the domestic or the foreign front. Ebert had unwittingly started the legend of the "stab in the back." While its troops had held a world coalition of enemies at bay, this legend insisted, treason had collapsed the state they were defending. Ebert and his government became its first victims, for they inherited a revolution they had not begun, a revolution they sought to moderate but ended by aborting. They became associated with a protracted period of domestic instability, and on them rested the onus of accepting the treaty of peace. No wonder the republic they founded would have a short life.

The first government of the Weimar regime consisted entirely of Socialists, both moderates and radicals. It created no soviet state. Now that they had their republic, some of its members were not sure they wanted it. What they did want and what Germany needed was domestic tranquility, and they did not hesitate to employ the remnants of the old imperial army to preserve it. The Russian Revolution of 1917 was not to be reenacted on German soil.

While the Bolshevik coup has remained the model against which the actions of the German Socialists have been measured, it is an inappropriate comparison. Lenin inherited a land with a deeply dissatisfied peasant majority and with an urban proletariat suffering degrees of exploitation unknown to the German worker. Germany's rural population, by contrast, burned no manors and seized no estates. German workers chiefly feared unemployment and the loss of high wartime wages which came with peace. The preconditions for radical revolution simply did not exist.

On the other hand, Lenin's government had the advantage of wrestling with its demons in the barely accessible interior of a Eurasian continental empire. Germany's industrial heartland, the most likely scene of revolutionary extremism, was a short train ride from Paris. Drastic experiments in social revolution would merely once more set in motion the Allied advance halted by the armistice and lead to the occupation of Germany.[17] German Socialists, even factions well to the left of

14

Ebert and his supporters, shrank from imposing a revolution which would have put an end to Germany as a sovereign state. They placed Germany's future in the hands of a democratically elected National Assembly which represented all major political elements from the Marxist left to the monarchist right. The assembly gave Germany a republican and democratic constitution, ended political inequities in state government, enfranchised women, and strengthened the federal government at the expense of the states. Only social reform remained on the agenda of an uncertain future.

Ebert's moderation did not prevent a peace whose provisions still arouse, even among Germans born generations after its signing, the most impassioned dissent. Foreign policy was a field in which Socialist influence remained weakest, even while Socialists ran the government. In December of 1918 Count Ulrich von Brockdorff-Rantzau (1869–1928), minister to Denmark under William II, became Secretary of State for Foreign Affairs. In April of the following year, he led the German delegation to Paris where he vainly pleaded for a moderation of the treaty. His ineptness as a negotiator, under admittedly difficult conditions, ruined what few chances there were to reduce the burdens of defeat. His weapon was public denunciation, a blunt tool in diplomacy, especially for the powerless.[18]

Signing the treaty of Versailles defeated the Socialists in the first election held in 1920 under the new constitution. For the next nine years, the democratic republic was governed by men who owed their careers to the empire. Although many of them, such as Foreign Minister Gustav Stresemann (1878–1929), served both ably and loyally, they dissociated themselves from the policies of the 1918–1919 interlude and remained indifferent to Germany's new constitutional democracy. They perpetuated a national policy of delusion in which rejection of Versailles remained the major article of faith. In diplomacy their stubbornness celebrated few victories, but that fact does not truly measure Germany's ability to arouse sympathy throughout the world for the real and imagined sufferings which he treaty was said to have caused. Even after Hitler had come and gone, the settlement's presumed injustices remained the most commonly cited major cause for his rise.

To the historian, the German case suffers from its unconditional nature. No treaty could be as bad as the Germans painted the Treaty of Versailles. After duly agreeing that it was signed under duress, that the failure to resolve the reparations issue in Paris was a tactical blunder,[19] and that the inclusion of a clause assigning Germany the guilt for starting the war was a psychological misstep,[20] one must remind the reader that

15

the treaty also redressed past injustices. Any glance at an ethnic map of Europe reveals that Germany's new boundaries harmonized to a greater degree with the principle of national self-determination than had her old ones. The maligned Polish Corridor contained a large majority of Poles, and even the controversial establishment of Danzig as a free city under the League of Nations conformed to Woodrow Wilson's Fourteen Points which had persuaded Germany to surrender. If the majority of Alsatians and Lorrainers, once more ceded to France, spoke German, it remained equally true that they gladly surrendered their German citizenship. The new boundary with Denmark was scrupulously ethnic.

At the same time, the historical debate must transcend right and wrong lest it obscure the fundamental issue of Germany's inability to come to terms with the fact of defeat. Under existing circumstances, no peace treaty was acceptable unless it declared that Germany's armies had won the war after all. Until that psychopathic yearning had been satisfied, the nation remained at war with the domestic and the international order—both products of an event which Germany insisted had not or at least should not have happened.

The collective rejection of reality paved the way for Hitler whose character and whose policies personified rejection. It renders pointless any debate about what might have saved the Weimar Republic and even more questionable any general conclusions derived from its early fall. That first experiment in republican democracy proved too fleeting to provide any stable indications about German devotion to political liberty.

Weimar's break with a well-established past held enormous risks. Germany led a day-by-day, hand-to-mouth existence resulting from defeat and associated with foreign pressure. Germans believed that sinister foreign interests propped up the "November [1918] regime"; their neighbors actually did little to enhance the republic's domestic popularity. For this reason, the part which the Depression played in Germany's fall must not be exaggerated. Every European country felt the economic jolt of the stock market crash of 1929. Only one sought refuge in the arms of a Hitler. It was the country which conducted military maneuvers with cardboard tanks and with nothing more formidable than machine guns and divisional artillery.

Hitler knew his Germans. After the swearing in of his first cabinet in the late morning of January 30, 1933, the new Chancellor returned to his suite at the Hotel Kaiserhof, accompanied by just one member of the new government, Minister of Defense General Werner von Blomberg. With his uncanny feel for effective poses, the new Chancellor understood what the moment required: a reassuring signal to hesitant conservatives and fence-sitting patriots. It was provided by putting on display the one active general in the government. What the curious onlookers on the sidewalks of Berlin did not know was the subject of conversation between the two: immediate German rearmament. Soon German armies would practice with real tanks, and by then thousands of workers, who had built them, would have exchanged the dole for regular paychecks.

Behind the public performance, the regime's unutterable sleaziness, brutality, and nihilism remained concealed from a far from inquisitive public mind. It is doubtful that Hitler would have been appointed Chancellor at all had he not been blackmailing President von Hindenburg's son, who seems to have embezzled money intended for agricultural subsidies and who is said to have pressed his father to appoint the Nazi Führer in order to escape exposure. This backstairs prelude set the tone for the government's treatment of other competitors and adversaries. The purge of Nazi storm troop leaders in June 1934 was officially justified by the Führer's ostensibly shocked discovery of their homosexual preferences. In 1938 Blomberg himself was dropped, after marriage to a former prostitute.

When blackmail or foul gossip furnished no pretext, force took its place. With Hitler's advent, Germany was engulfed by waves of terror. Arresting, torturing, and killing persons for their beliefs became, for the first time since the religious wars, a commonplace German public policy. It is worth remembering that Germans, who never gave Hitler a clear mandate in a free election, became the first victims of his bloodlust. Socialists, Communists, Catholics and Conservatives died by the thousands. The great dress rehearsal for Jewish and Slav extermination took place on German soil and was practiced on German victims. In the course of this ghastly preparation, the active political opposition was executed or permanently silenced in concentration camps. Hitler's revolutionary vanguard made its own study of Leninist and Stalinist models and agreed that the best way to overcome political opposition was to exterminate it.

Amidst this moral collapse, national morale was maintained by methods whose horror dawned only gradually upon a nation long unaccustomed to coping with reality. Opponents were skillfully divided into small and vulnerable groups. Not everyone believed the Jews to be at the root of all of Germany's woes as the Nazi slogan, "Die Juden sind unser Unglück," insisted. But the Jews constituted less than one percent of Germany's population; an injustice to so diminutive a group appeared a small price to pay for national and economic revival, especially to those who did not have to pay it. Political enemies on the left could be similarly isolated by tarring them with the brush of treason, if Communist; the charge of fomenting class war, if Socialist. Opponents on the right, from priests to army officers, were more easily disarmed by unsubstantiated charges of sexual perversion and depravity, as has already been indicated.

Meanwhile the state rearmed. Work was provided for the unemployed, though there were fewer and fewer goods to buy with their pay. And the timid were overwhelmed with a succession of diplomatic victories. Compulsory military service was restored, the demilitarized sectors along the country's western border were reoccupied, and limitation of naval armament reduced. Finally, in 1938, a restored Germany pushed beyond its own borders when Hitler reunited Austria, the land of his birth, with Germany.

IV

The Führer's triumphal entry into Vienna seemed to end uncertainties which went back to 1866. Since the separation from Germany, the Habsburg monarchy had not only slowly lost the allegiance of its Magyar and Slav subjects, many of its 10 million Germans cast envious glances in the direction of the victorious northern empire in which their nation constituted the majority. As Vienna, in particular, became a melting pot of nations, a growing number of Austrian Germans became convinced that their cultural identity could only survive in conjunction with an exclusively German state.

Had Germany won the First World War, an Austro-German *Grossdeutschland* might well have been the result, reducing the Habsburg emperor to an innocuous proconsulship over a remnant of Balkan satellites. But Germany, to the consternation of its citizens, was defeated, and by the time her armistice was signed, the last of the Habsburgs had abdicated, leaving the nationalities of his empire to make their own pact with the future. In Vienna the German rump of the *Reichsrat*, the Imperial Parliament, proclaimed a republic of "German Austria." Thirteen days later the government of that republic resolved unanimously to merge with Germany. It did so with the support of its citizens, but it had reckoned without the outside world. Allied statesmen sought to reduce German power, not expand it, and therefore insisted that Austria remain an independent state.

INTRODUCTION

Austrians bore the cross of self-government unwillingly. They faced prohibitive economic problems, largely a result of new state boundaries which separated them from traditional markets and sources of supply. Independence also posed formidable territorial challenges. For a time the question "What is Austria?" was as difficult to answer as "What is Germany?" had been in 1848. Three million Germans scattered throughout predominantly Czech Bohemia and Moravia wanted to remain subjects of Vienna. The prospects of the resulting territorial monstrosity did as much as Czech interposition to deny their wish. Yugoslavia's claim on Klagenfurt in Carinthia, on the other hand, was settled by plebiscite in favor of Austria, as was the fate of the Transleithanian Germans of Hungary. After a referendum in December 1921, their entire home province (*Burgenland*), except the district of Ödenburg (Sopron), was transferred to Austria. Meanwhile, the inhabitants of Austria's westernmost province, Vorarlberg, had voted overwhelmingly to join Switzerland, only to be rebuffed by the federal government in Berne. As late as the spring of 1921, the Tirol and the province of Salzburg held local plebiscites which indicated that the majority of their inhabitants desired union with Germany. But this option remained closed.[21]

The Austrian Republic was propped up by foreign loans, surrounded by hostile neighbors, and only fitfully encouraged by platonic friendship gestures from Berlin and Rome. In 1931 Germany offered Austria a custom's union to soften the blows of the Great Depression. France and her East European allies, Czechoslovakia, Poland, and Yugoslavia, successfully opposed the economic integration of the two German states.

Domestically, the rump republic remained divided in other ways. Two-party systems are not invariably the boon Anglo-Saxons claim. In Vienna, a Socialist and a Catholic Party found loyal collaboration difficult. The red capital, though almost one out of three Austrians lived within its corporate limits, was tossed in a stormy sea of black (i.e., clerical) distrust verging on hate. In 1934, a clerical government used rifle and cannon to crush Socialism but found itself almost immediately confronted by an attempted Nazi coup. Only a mobilization of Italian troops on the Brenner prevented a second bloodbath within one year.

Now, four years later, Nazi Germany, economically recovered, rearmed, and allied with Mussolini's Italy, could declare its relations with the German brothers south of the Alps to be a domestic problem and occupied Austria without asking anyone's consent. Everyone in Europe whose opinion mattered seemed to agree that Hitler had terminated an unnatural separation, and the Austrians themselves welcomed the German troops enthusiastically.

But prolonged and passionate courtships often lead to short marriages.[22] Austro-German union failed, because it was the work of a man whose personal happiness seems to have depended on causing suffering, who would exploit man's dark side, but who disregarded his noble traits. Thus, Hitler understood the expectations of material gain, but he remained deaf to the idealistic elements represented by Austrian Pan-Germanism. His government developed Austrian resources, notably electric power, steel, and oil. Politically, on the other hand, the Führer relegated his homeland to the role of a provincial backwater. Austrians gradually discovered that their dream of German solidarity was not Hitler's dream. He merely used it, and them, to pursue conquests which exceeded the reach of Greater Germany, just as the demands of World War I had exceeded the joint capacities of the Hohenzollern and Habsburg empire.

What were these dreams; what were these plans? Despite the profusion of evidence and the torrent of documents, memoirs, and monographs pouring down every year from inexhaustible reservoirs of scholarship, they remain a mystery. We know what Hitler did, but we do not know why. He wrote few personal letters; he had no personal friends to whom he unburdened his soul at any time in his life; and he left no diaries and no memoirs.[23] The few personal recollections in *Mein Kampf*, his rather unreadable and verbose major campaign tract, have been revealed to be mostly lies.

This leaves a puzzled and shocked world with much that cannot be explained. After the annexation of Austria and the annexation of the German-speaking areas of Czechoslovakia, Hitler had outdone Bismarck. Why was it necessary within six months to pounce on Poland? And why did Hitler decide to invade the USSR only a month after the astonishing defeat of France in 1940? What real or imaginary necessity prompted him to declare war against the United States, after Japan had attacked Pearl Harbor without giving Germany advance notice?

Was the touted new Germanic empire of the German nation, including Dutchmen, Flemings, Danes and Norwegians, a serious objective or merely a propaganda gimmick? If it were a game, did Hitler play as false with ardent National Socialists, like Heinrich Himmler, as he did with his foreign adversaries? If it were a goal which he pursued seriously, how could he imagine that his empire could be founded in a vast territory most of whose populations had been either slaughtered or reduced by Assyrian levels of slavery? Could it be that all his mutually inconsistent and fleeting projects were indeed a mere accompaniment to one single purpose: extermination of the Jews? For in their case alone, Nazi

INTRODUCTION

Germany seemed to possess a consistent policy. They were imprisoned, evacuated, shot, and gassed wherever German armies seized control.[24]

Enigma or not, Hitler had captured the German nation and held it enthralled until his suicide on the afternoon of April 30, 1945. In the iron grasp of his illusions, Germans were forced out of their cocoon of self-deception. No amount of national pride or Hitlerian rhetoric protected the German soldier against the Russian winter, stayed the bombs dropped by fleets of British and American planes, or shortened the casualty lists. In the end, no alibi remained to sustain the most cherished illusions. Long before final defeat overtook them, the Germans, who had ravaged every region of Europe, became everyone's prey. From large, amply equipped armies and increasingly well-supplied guerilla forces to individual saboteurs removing bolts from railway ties and stringing wires across highways, everyone turned on the century's great tormentor.

When Red Army tanks battered down the defenses of East Prussia's capital of Königsberg,[25] planning for Russia's colonization had become academic. Now Russians colonized instead of Germans. East Prussia, not the Ukraine, became the colony.

Bestiality dominated the war on the eastern front when the Germans were victors. It continued to set the tone after they had become victims. Russian armored columns ploughed through lines of screaming refugees, avenging not only their own dead but those hapless hosts in the streets of Rotterdam and on the highways of France on whom German armor and aircraft had visited similar tortures in 1940. At last, an unnecessarily massive Anglo-American air attack laid Dresden in ruins, burying thousands of civilians under the rubble of its baroque splendors.

Surrender in the west was more civilized[26] but no less total. From the capitulation of Aachen on October 21, 1944, to the last day of fighting in Austria on May 7, Germans exchanged the status of citizenship in a sovereign state for imprisonment or dependence.[27]

In the final act, the Third Reich collapsed totally and ingloriously. Cornered, its leadership surrendered, disappeared, or committed suicide—in Hitler's case, with a curse on his lips.[28] Some, like Foreign Minister Joachim von Ribbentrop and the Reichsführer—SS Heinrich Himmler, attempted a last-minute accommodation with the enemy.[29] None chose death in combat, though all at one time or another had urged their compatriots to fight to the last man and to fire until the last bullet had been spent. The final announcement from Berlin, on May 1 that Hitler had died fighting at his command post, only proved that a regime which began with blackmail signed off with a lie.

V

On April 30, what was left of Germany? Little territory, no resources to sustain its armies, no values to cherish or to defend. Under the strain of tyranny, national unity, too, had slowly disintegrated. For the first time in German history, thousands of citizens left their homeland to escape political persecution.[30] For the first time, Germans actually debated whether or not a patriotic duty to overthrow the government existed.[31] In the desolation of Russian prison camps, the "Free Germany Committee" and an association of German Officers, chaired by the descendant of one of Frederick the Great's most renowned lieutenants, began in September of 1943 to call for an immediate peace and the overthrow of Hitler. Regardless of the uses to which the Soviet Union put them, these two groups contained few Communists and consisted of men who knew that the "war was lost" but wanted to keep "Germany from being lost as well."[32] With approaching defeat, regime supporters prepared to change uniform, and each tried to save his individual skin at a comrade's expense.[33]

National demoralization ran so deep that in the end nothing changed. Adolf Hitler with his "silver-decorated uniform" of "a street car conductor," and a face which "bore the stigma of sexual inadequacy" and expressed "the rancour of the half-man who had turned . . . his impotence into [a rationale for] brutalizing others," represented to the last a legitimate authority from which Germans dared not free themselves.[34] They remained loyal to a man who did not know what loyalty was. They served to the last a leader, who, unlike Friedrich Ebert, did not hesitate to risk the destruction of Germany.

Once again the decisive push, the inspiration and the design for change came from abroad. Once again Germany would have to be made over without German initiative. The demand for unconditional surrender and the Allied plan for dividing the country into zones of occupation both postulated the end of the sovereign nation. Throughout the last year of the war, everyone, from Stalin to minuscule resistance and exile organizations, contributed a blueprint of Germany's future, except the Germans.[35]

"What is to become of a thoroughly coarsened people," an anguished German Conservative asked in his diary on August 16, 1944.[36] On May 8, 1945, several weeks after this particular dissenter had been executed at Dachau concentration camp, his country's third collapse in less than 150 years placed the burden of an answer on the shoulders of Britain, the Soviet Union, and the United States.

22

INTRODUCTION

The papers that follow discuss how the Soviet Union and the U.S. discharged their disproportionately large responsibilities. They reveal how U.S. and Soviet roles in Germany affected their attitudes toward each other and how they defended their respective interests in the Central European theater as world powers and as Germany's and Austria's guides to an uncertain future.

NOTES

1. In 1697 the Elector of Saxony became King of Poland; four years later the Elector of Brandenburg received permission to call himself King in the former Polish fief of Prussia. In 1714 the Elector of Hanover succeeded to the throne of the Stuarts in England, while the Landgrave of Hesse-Cassel, Frederick I, married the sister of Charles XII of Sweden and succeeded his brother-in-law in 1720.
2. Owen Connelly, *Napoleon's Satellite Kingdoms* (New York, 1965), p. 299.
3. Cf. Section VI of the Constitution of 1848 in Ernst Rudolf Huber, ed., *Quellen zum Staatsrecht der Neuzeit* (Tübingen, 1949), I, 257–63, with F.-A. Helie, ed., *Les constitutions de la France* (Paris, 1879), pp. 270–71.
4. The two strands must remain distinct, because they differed and often conflicted. A chronicle of their relationship has recently been attempted in John L. Snell and Hans A. Schmitt, *The Democratic Movement in Germany, 1789–1914* (Chapel Hill, N.C., 1976); see particularly pp. 77–129 on the problems of 1848.
5. As claimed by Otto Hintze in his preface to *Die Hohenzollern und ihr Werk. Fünfhundert Jahre vaterländischer Geschichte* (Berlin, 1915), p. *vi.*
6. First among them Helmuth Boehme, *Deutschlands Weg zur Grossmacht: Studien zum Verhältnis von Wirtschaft und Staat während der Reichsgründungszeit 1848–1881* (Cologne, 1966), pp. 116–229.
7. Cf. Friedrich Zunkel, *Der Rheinisch-Westfälische Unternehmer 1834–1879. Ein Beitrag zur Geschichte des Deutschen Bürgertums im 19. Jahrhundert* (Dortmunder Schriften zur Sozialforschung, Vol. 19) (Cologne, 1962), pp. 28–29, 218–29.
8. Readers dependent on works in English should consult Michael Stürmer, "Bismarck in Perspective," *Central European History* 4 (1971):291–331, and my critique of his assessments in "Bismarck as Seen from the Nearest Church Steeple," ibid., 6 (1973):363–69, with Stürmer's perplexed rejoinder, ibid., 369–72.
9. For a thoughtful analysis of this transformation, see Elisabeth Fehrenbach, *Wandlungen des deutschen Kaisergedankens* (Studien

zur Geschichte des neunzehnten Jahrhunderts, Vol. 1) (Munich, 1969), especially pp. 89–124, 226–30.

10. Snell and Schmitt, *Democratic Movement in Germany*, p. 362.

11. Ludwig Thomas, *Gesammelte Werke*, 4 vols. (Munich, 1927), *I*, 570.

12. For a good summary of both problems, see Oswald Hauser, "Polen und Dänen im Deutschen Reich," in Theodor Schieder and Ernst Deuerlein, eds., *Reichsgründung 1870–71: Tatsachen, Kontroverse, Interpretationen* (Stuttgart, 1970), pp. 291–309.

13. The standard treatment in English of this difficult relationship is Dan P. Silverman's *Reluctant Union: Alsace-Lorraine and Imperial Germany, 1871–1918* (University Park, Pa., 1972), and for one of the most dramatic explosions of mutual dislike, Richard W. Mackay, "The Zabern Affair, 1913–1914" (Ph.D. diss., University of California, Los Angeles, 1967). Jean-Marie Mayeur's judicious *Autonomie et politique en Alsace. La constitution de 1911* (Paris, 1970), explains why the reforms on the eve of World War I provided so little relief.

14. Ernst Toller, *I was a German* (New York, 1934), p. 67.

15. Collected in such contemporaneous and posthumous volumes as Harold Morré, ed., *20 Jahre S.M. Heiter Bilder zu ernsten Ereignissen* (Berlin, 1909), and Friedrich Wendel, *Wilhelm II. in der Karikatur* (Dresden, 1928).

16. Quoted from James Joll, *The Second International, 1889–1914* (London, 1955), p. 176.

17. Cf. Arno J. Mayer, *Politics and Diplomacy of Peacemaking. Containment and Counterrevolution at Versailles, 1918–1919* (New York, 1967), pp. 229–83. The fear of Allied reaction to possible Sovietization also affected the course of the revolution at the state level, notably in Bavaria and in Baden with its common border with France.

18. E.g. Heinrich Euler, *Die Aussenpolitik der Weimarer Republik 1918–1923 vom Waffenstillstand bis zum Ruhrkonflikt* (Aschaffenburg, 1957), pp. 91–111; Udo Wengst, *Graf Brockdorff-Rantzau und die aussenpolitischen Anfänge der Weimarer Republik* (Moderne Geschichte und Politik, Vol. 2) (Berne, 1973), and for a telling exposé of Germany's inflexible attitude toward the peace, Peter Krüger, *Deutschland und die Reparationen 1918–19: Die Genesis des Reparationsproblems in Deutschland zwischen Waffenstillstand und Versailler Friedensschluss* (Schriftenreihe der Vierteljahreshefte für Zeitgeschichte, Vol. 25) (Stuttgart, 1973).

19. Though there was no indication of Allied determination to bleed Germany forever, as was often maintained, recent debates among young American historians remind us that German complaints must be taken with a grain of salt in other respects as well. See Sally Marks, "Reparations Reconsidered: A Reminder," *Central European*

INTRODUCTION

History 2 (1969):356–65; David Felix, "Reparations Reconsidered with a Vengeance," ibid., 4 (1971):171–79; and Sally Marks, "Reparations Reconsidered: A Rejoinder," ibid., 5 (1972):358–61.

20. Though not necessarily an historical injustice. See Fritz Fischer, *Krieg der Illusionen, die deutsche Politik von 1911 bis 1914* (Düsseldorf, 1970).

21. The scholarly returns on many of these issues remain fragmentary. On the German areas in Czechoslovakia see the excellent map in Victor S. Mamatey and Radomir Luža, eds., *A History of the Czechoslovak Republic, 1918–1948* (Princeton, 1973), p. 238. While the Carinthian border question awaits a dispassionate chronicler, Jon D. Berlin's "The United States and the Burgenland," *Austrian History Yearbook* 8 (1972):39–58, provides some admirable insights into the complexities of that question. On Vorarlberg and Switzerland see Horst Zimmermann, *Die Schweiz und Österreich wärend der Zwischenkriegszeit. Eine Studie und Dokumentation internationaler Beziehungen im Schatten der Grossmächte* (Wiesbaden, 1973), pp. 88–137.

22. See the eloquent testimonial of the documents collected by Karl Stadler, *Österreich 1938–1945 im Spiegel der NS-Akten* (Vienna, 1966), and the events chronicled in Radomir Luža, *Austro-German Relations in the Anschluss Era* (Princeton, 1975).

23. What little survives of personal documents, and it is inconclusive enough, has been collected in Werner Maser, *Hitler's Briefe und Notizen. Sein Weltbild in handschriftlichen Dokumenten* (Düsseldorf, 1973).

24. Anyone seeking answers to these still unanswerable questions should begin with Norman Rich's magisterial and comprehensive *Hitler's War Aims: The Establishment of the New Order* (New York, 1974), which covers all fronts and which shows as clearly as the evidence allows who exterminated whom in what section of conquered Europe.

25. Fritz Gause, *Die Geschichte der Stadt Königsberg in Preussen*, 3 vols. (Cologne and Vienna, 1968–71), *III*, 170–77.

26. Which did not keep a German Air Force officer in June 1945 from complaining to this writer about the unceremonious manner in which American troops closed the last headquarters of the Luftwaffe and carted away to prison its portly and ever resplendent *Reichsmarschall*.

27. Werner Haupt, *Das Ende im Westen, 1945* (Dorheim/Hesse, 1972), pp. 30–31, 177–81; Gabriele Hindinger, *Das Kriegsende und der Wiederaufbau demokratischer Verhältnisse in Oberösterreich im Jahre 1945* (Publikationen des Österreichischen Instituts für Zeitgeschichte der Universität Wien, Vol. 6) (Vienna, 1968), pp. 51–57; and Theo Rosiwall, *Die letzten Tage. Die militärische Besetzung Österreichs, 1945* (Vienna, 1969), pp. 303–19.

28. Cf. "Hitler's letzte Lagebesprechung," *Der Spiegel*, 10 January 1966, p. 44.

29. See Marlis G. Steinert, *23 Days: The Final Collapse of Nazi Germany*, trans. Richard Barry (New York, 1969), pp. 9–27.
30. Many personal family traditions in the United States notwithstanding, the German emigrant of the nineteenth century left for economic not political reasons. Cf. such general surveys of the phenomenon as Peter Marschalck's *Deutsche Überseewanderung im 19. Jahrhundert* (Industrielle Welt, Vol. 14) (Stuttgart, 1973), esp. pp. 54–59, and the careful case study by Wolf-Heino Struck, *Die Auswanderung aus dem Herzogtum Nassau (1806–1866)* (Geschichtliche Landeskunde, Vol. 4) (Wiesbaden, 1966).
31. There is a large literature on the German resistance, larger than that resistance itself. Hans Rothfels' sympathetic account published soon after the war, *The German Resistance Against Hitler* (Chicago, 1949), remains the best introduction to the subject.
32. *Deutsche Wohin? Protokoll der Gründungsversammlung des National-Komitees Freies Deutschland und des Deutschen Offiziersbundes* (Mexico, D.F., 1944), p. 20.
33. For a particularly graphic example taken from the final days of Nazi occupation in Norway, see Willy Brandt, *In Exile: Essays, Reflections and Letters, 1933–1947*, trans. R. W. Last (London, 1971), p. 107.
34. Quoted from Friedrich Percyval Reck-Malleczewen, *Diary of a Man in Despair*, trans. Paul Rubens (London, 1970), pp. 23, 75.
35. Two major studies of unconditional surrender document the soundness of the policy dogma: Paul Kecskemeti, *Strategic Surrender: The Politics of Victory and Defeat* (Stanford, Ca., 1958), pp. 216–23; and Maxime Mourin, *Reddition sans conditions* (Paris, 1973), pp. 323–39. Anne Armstrong, *Unconditional Surrender: The Impact of the Casablanca Policy upon World War II* (New Brunswick, N.J., 1961), passim, registers some secondary practical reservations which fail to point to major alternatives. On the negotiations of zonal boundaries, see Tony Sharp, *The Wartime Alliance and the Zonal Division* (Oxford, 1975), while Winifred N. Hadsel, "What Kind of Peace with Germany—Terms Proposed by Liberated Nations of Europe," *Foreign Policy Reports* XX, no. 17:210–19, presents an interesting contemporary review of proposals for Germany's future.
36. Reck-Malleczewen, *Diary*, p. 198.

2

The Formulation and Initial Implementation of U.S. Occupation Policy in Germany

Earl F. Ziemke
University of Georgia

United States occupation policy in Germany during the years 1945 to 1950 had three fundamental purposes: administrative, social, and political. However, these purposes were not always mutually compatible nor mutually consistent. The *administrative* focus imposed a requirement to conduct military government in a defeated country in accordance with international law and decent administrative practice and to do so with economy of resources and effort. The *social* focus evolved from an assumption that during the two world wars and the Nazi period Germany exhibited certain dangerous national character traits. The need for social reorientation was beyond question; the forms it could take, however, were various as were the amounts of time and effort required. The *political* focus made it necessary to plan a restoration of Germany to the national world community it had long disrupted and to do so at a time when a new international rift was developing. The resulting combination depended upon how the three purposes were perceived at a given time by the White House, the War Department, the State Department, other governmental departments and agencies, the quadripartite control organizations, the theater command, the field commands, and press and public opinion.

U.S. OCCUPATION IN EUROPE

When the war against Germany ended in May 1945, United States occupation policy was embodied in a document entitled "Directive to the Commander in Chief of U.S. Forces of Occupation Regarding the Military Government of Germany in the Period Immediately Following the Cessation of Organized Resistance (Post Defeat)," or JCS 1067. Although it bore a Joint Chiefs of Staff number, JCS 1067 had been written by the War Department Civil Affairs Division and was based on consultations with Presidents Franklin D. Roosevelt and Harry S. Truman and conferences among the War, State, and Treasury Departments. With the concurrence of two presidents, the directive was endowed with a scriptural aura and was destined to be regarded as the key United States occupation document. Consequently, any analysis of occupation policy has to begin with JCS 1067.

The first version of JCS 1067 was drafted in September 1944, nine months before the war ended. The War Department, believing the German collapse to be imminent, expressed an urgent requirement for policy guidance. The War Department concern, while real, was also limited. Primarily on President Roosevelt's insistence, a long train of decisions reaching back to early 1942 had established that governing occupied territory was to be essentially a civilian task. The War Department had managed to preserve control for the army during a so-called "period of military necessity," that is, while the war was in progress and for a short military period after the German surrender or collapse. The War Department wanted the policy statement for a posthostilities military period, which was expected to last anywhere from a few weeks to several months. Hence the elaborate title. The words "Immediately Following the Cessation of Organized Resistance" established the policy as temporary. The words "Post Defeat" in parenthesis imposed an additional limitation.

Short as the military period might be, it appeared to the U.S. staffs in Europe and in Washington that the army would be courting disaster if it entered into the occupation without a policy guide. Ordinarily, such guidance would have been provided to the theater command from Washington as a matter of course. However, this was not the case for Germany. A number of agencies, among them the European Advisory Commission (EAC), the Combined Civil Affairs Committee (CCAC) of the Combined Chiefs of Staff (CCS), the Civil Affairs Division (CAD), the U.S. and British Control Council groups, and the Supreme Headquarters Allied Expeditionary Force (SHAEF) G-5, were working on the machinery for the postdefeat administration of Germany, but none had the authority to make policy. Since the occupation was scheduled

28

to be tripartite, the European Advisory Commission, an American-British-Soviet body sitting in London, could have been the ultimate instrument for formulating policy. The EAC, however, was enmeshed in a long-standing intergovernmental dispute over where policy should be made, in Washington or in London. In Washington, the EAC was unacceptable as a policy source. The Combined Civil Affairs Committee, as an organ of the Combined Chiefs of Staff in SHAEF's direct line of command, was the agency that must approve and transmit any guidelines sent to General Dwight D. Eisenhower as long as the combined command in Europe existed. However, the CCAC was based in Washington and also caught up in the competition between Washington and London. From the War Department point of view, the administration of Germany must not be initiated in a policy vacuum. Thus, it appeared necessary to produce a U.S. statement that would supply a technically workable basis for the occupation's military interim.

Drafted in response to this need, JCS 1067 might have remained what it started out to be—an improvisation designed to fill a small administrative gap. But other events intervened. In late August of 1944, Secretary of the Treasury Henry J. Morganthau, Jr. returned from a trip to Europe and brought a copy of a handbook for military government written in the SHAEF G-5 German Country Unit. Having nothing else to go by, the SHAEF planners had assumed that the military government's mission would be to provide the Germans with conventional good government. On August 26 the handbook arrived via the White House at Secretary of War Henry L. Stimson's office. With it were critical comments by Morganthau and a note from the President that began, "This so-called Handbook is pretty bad. If it has not been sent out . . . all copies should be withdrawn. . . ." The President added that it was of utmost importance "this time" that everybody in Germany should recognize that Germany was a defeated nation. He did not propose to start "a WPA, PWA, or CCC for Germany," and the German people were to "have it driven home that the whole nation has been engaged in a lawless conspiracy against the decencies of modern civilization."[1]

On September 2, in the first meeting of a newly formed Cabinet Committee on Germany, consisting of the Secretaries of State, War, and Treasury and their chief advisors, the Treasury representatives presented the Morgenthau Plan for Germany. Based on the assumption that Germany was an incorrigible instigator of world wars, the plan proposed to deny Germany the means for building armies by tearing down industrial plants, sealing coal mines, and converting the Germans into a nation of small farmers. Secretary of War Stimson opposed the plan, saying he saw "enormous general evils coming from it," and the committee adopted a five-point program for Germany.[2] The points, none of which originated in the Morgenthau Plan were: demilitarization; dissolution of the Nazi Party; controls over communications, press, propaganda, and education; reparation for those countries wanting it; and decentralization of the German governmental structure. The main feature of the Morgenthau Plan, the deindustrialization of Germany, euphemistically called pastoralization, was not included. Two weeks later, however, the plan and specifically that part of it received the President's and Prime Minister Winston S. Churchill's approval at the Quebec Conference.

When State, War, and Treasury Department representatives sat down in the office of Assistant Secretary of War John J. McCloy on September 22 to draft the document that was to become JCS 1067, the Treasury Department could claim a key role in the policy-making for Germany. Its approach was predominantly social, namely, to eliminate the Germans as a threat to world peace by converting them into a subsistence-level agrarian people. The War Department's concern was still short-term administration, but the President's reaction to the handbook had had its effect. While Secretary Stimson was still campaigning against the Morgenthau Plan and would, in fact, in a few days have the satisfaction of having Mr. Roosevelt tell him that Morgenthau had "pulled a boner," McCloy was apparently convinced that any suspicion of "softness" toward the Germans would raise another storm in the White House.[3] The result was a document that could and was meant to be interpreted several different ways.

The content of JCS 1067 was essentially an expansion of the Cabinet Committee's five-point program and contained nothing that had not been proposed before. Demilitarization and dissolution of the Nazi Party had been called for in the Atlantic Charter of August 1941. A limit on relief supplies for Germany to the minimum necessary to prevent disease and disorder threatening the health and safety of the occupation troops dated back almost a year to the original planning for the invasion of northwestern Europe. It had seemed, then, that some strict limits had to be set on relief supplies to prevent the Allied forces from becoming a gigantic welfare agency. The disease and disorder formula had also been applied in a slightly less stringent form to the liberated countries. The economic section of the directive came closer to echoing the Morgenthau Plan. It prohibited German economic rehabilitation or steps designed to maintain or strengthen the German economy, but it, too, had originated outside the Treasury Department. In August, Eisenhower had asked to be relieved of responsibility for sustaining the German economy because he believed the country was going to be too much of a burned-out wreck for him to handle.[4] Probably JCS 1067 most satisfied Morgenthau in what it did not do, namely, it did not specify any positive program and left the door open to the pastoralization he envisaged. In the War Department view, the omission was appropriate to a short-term directive that would not prejudice whatever policy might finally be agreed upon.

JCS 1067 received President Roosevelt's approval on September 29, 1944 and became the official statement of United States policy. Thus, it began its long career as the most controversial occupation document. To the War Department, its main defender, JCS 1067 became extremely valuable as the agreed and approved policy directive and the only one likely to achieve that status, since the President subsequently announced that he did not believe in making policy for a country before it was occupied. Elsewhere—in the State Department, particularly, but also in European military government organizations—JCS 1067 would be seen primarily as a slightly veiled version of the Morgenthau Plan. Walter L. Dorn, who knew the occupation well, would still describe it a dozen years later as "largely a Treasury document."[5] From the outset, it had practically no chance of becoming combined policy, not because of the supposed Morgenthau influence, but because it came into competition with a British policy paper in the Combined Civil Affairs Committee whose influence, in effect, cancelled it out. When the War Department finally prevailed upon the State Department to forward it to the European Advisory Commission for adoption as tripartite policy, James W. Riddleberger, the chief of the Division of Central European Affairs, recommended that the U.S. representatives in the EAC be advised "not to insist on JCS 1067 to the point where it will unduly prolong negotiations."[6] In March 1945, JCS 1067 almost died when the State Department secured the President's "OK FDR" on a draft directive of its own.

The existence of two directives forced another round of discussion among the State, War, and Treasury Departments that culminated in a meeting on the morning of March 23 where the two were amalgamated into a single policy statement. The bulk of JCS 1067 survived—but with changes. Policy established by the four-power Control Council for Germany (France had been added as an occupying power) would be paramount, and the U.S. zone commander would exercise his authority in accordance with directives from his own government only in the absence of such policy. As a result, JCS 1067 would apply only if the Control Council did not formulate other policy. The zone commander would not be responsible for regulating and sustaining the German economy, but he would see to it that the German authorities under him did so "to the fullest extent possible."[7] The President initialed the statement that afternoon and added a paragraph which read: "Germany's ruthless warfare and fanatical Nazi resistance have destroyed the German economy and made chaos and suffering inevitable. The Germans cannot escape responsibility for what they have brought upon themselves."[8] Later, those two sentences would epitomize the Morgenthau Plan in the minds of the Germans, but at the time, Secretary of the Treasury Morgenthau disclaimed authorship and saw no significance in the lines, other than their being "pretty good propaganda."[9]

While JCS 1067 was being rewritten to incorporate the new decisions, the presidency passed to Harry S. Truman. During his first weeks in office, Mr. Truman was not inclined to upset the policies of his predecessor. But, he was much less set in his opinions on the occupation than President Roosevelt had been. He let it be known early that he did not agree with the Morgenthau Plan, and before the final version of JCS 1067 went to Eisenhower in May, he approved an amendment allowing Eisenhower to keep German aluminum, magnesium, and synthetic oil and rubber plants operating to meet the needs of the occupation forces.

The Treasury influence in occupation planning waned rapidly in the spring of 1945; nevertheless, JCS 1067 still appeared to bear the imprint of the Morgenthau Plan. Lieutenant General Lucius D. Clay, Eisenhower's Deputy Military Governor for Germany, was dismayed at the rigidity of the economic provisions. In one of his first letters from Europe, Clay asked Major General John H. Hilldring, the director of the War Department Civil Affairs Division, for a more "flexible and general" directive.[10] Reiterating the War Department's predominant interest in administrative propriety, Hilldring replied that he expected final policy to "bubble up" from the facts Clay would discover, but it would not be in the army's or Clay's interest to have Clay formulate policy. JCS 1067, Hilldring added, put the U.S. government behind the occupation; and without it, Clay's greatest problem might be "the flanking fire" that would fall on him from U.S. sources.[11]

After the German surrender, JCS 1067 was official U.S. policy for the German occupation, but it was not in force anywhere in Germany. General Eisenhower, who would come under the directive as Military Governor of the U.S. zone, was still Supreme Commander Allied Expeditionary Force (SCAEF). In that capacity his command channel was through the Combined Chiefs of Staff, not the U.S. Joint Chiefs of Staff, and the British contingent of the CCS was less likely to accept JCS 1067 as combined policy in 1945 than they had been in the fall of 1944. The directive was sent to the European Advisory Commission, but its chances of being accepted there were also slight. What Eisenhower had as policy for the combined command were two papers. One of those was CCS 551, which had been written in the spring of 1944 by the Combined Civil Affairs Committee as a directive for the period prior to defeat or surrender. Like JCS 1067, it called for de-Nazification and demilitarization and applied the disease and disorder limits to relief for Germany. On the other hand, it authorized Eisenhower to stock relief supplies for Germany on the same scale as for liberated countries. The economic section instructed him to assume full control over German industrial production and to integrate the German economy into the European and World economies.[12]

The second paper consisted of three points which in the aftermath of the handbook controversy the CCS had ordered affixed to the flyleaf of each copy of the SHAEF handbook for Germany. The first point prohibited "steps looking toward the economic rehabilitation of Germany" but simultaneously directed that the Germans be required to continue economic controls. Point two reiterated the disease and disorder relief formula, and the third point required the exclusion from public office of all active Nazis and "ardent" Nazi sympathizers.[13] Whether the three points constituted policy is debatable, since they were technically only an admonition to the working level of military government. The most visible piece of policy was nonfraternization. It had been mentioned in CCS 551 but had not been defined until September 1944, when President Roosevelt vehemently criticized news photographs showing American troops socializing with German civilians. Eisenhower then ordered all personnel under his command to abstain from any social contact with Germans of either sex and of any age.

Since the combined command, SHAEF, continued in existence to July 14, 1945, JCS 1067 remained in abeyance, allowing time for some revision of thinking on the policy. The Germans did not need to be shown they had lost the war; they knew it. Hence, demilitarization was no great problem. De-Nazification was a different case. The Nazi system was gone, but the task of determining who had been Nazis and "ardent" sympathizers remained. The disease and disorder conditions were so close to being met that SHAEF began importing 650,000 tons of wheat for Germany in June. As for industrial production, the threat was not one of a resurgent war industry but of total collapse. The Germans were not going to start marching again, but they could starve or become a permanent burden on U.S. taxpayers. From those stark possibilities, one new policy element rapidly evolved: treating Germany as a single economic unit. Another policy, nonfraternization, also disappeared.

Faced with the determined and ingenious resistance of his troops and a fast-rising venereal disease rate, Eisenhower let it die.

Meanwhile, JCS 1067 proved to be remarkably durable. On July 7 in expanded form, it became the military government directive for the U.S. Forced European Theater (USFET), and later in the month, much of its language was incorporated into the Potsdam Protocol. When it was declassified in early August, the Morgenthau Plan immediately assumed concrete significance in the minds of the Germans. In fact, however, the gap in JCS 1067 that could have accommodated the plan was no longer the potentially ominous void it had been. The Potsdam Conference had made hard decisions on reparations and expulsion of Germans from lands in which they had lived, in some instances, for centuries, but it had also determined to encourage the development of democratic political parties and to restore self-government at the local and state levels. Economic unification had been accepted as a principle, and President Truman had given the War Department responsibility for financing and procuring aid to Germany and specified that the program would apply to the U.S. zone whether or not a unified program was adopted for the whole country.

During the late summer of 1945, the occupation entered what has been called the Potsdam era, the period in which the United States attempted to get the German problem solved through four-power cooperation and economic unification. Against French and Soviet resistance, U.S. effort made virtually no headway, although it consumed vast amounts of energy. The effective area of U.S. activity was the zone, where new pressures came into play—among them the press and public opinion. One effort that demanded attention after the victory was the elimination of Nazism and the Nazis. How thoroughly that was done appeared to the U.S. public to be the best gauge of the occupation's success. The American people had not supported the Morgenthau Plan, but they did believe the Nazis should be brought to account; consequently, any mistakes on that score made good press copy. By October, enough controversy had been publicized to lead General Clay to undertake a clean sweep in de-Nazification. Military Government Law No. 8 of October 7 excluded Nazis and Nazi sympathizers from all government and private employment above the level of common laborer.

While the Germans were reeling under the shock of Law No. 8, other pressures on the military government caused the Germans to be pushed just as disconcertingly in a different direction. Concerned about the criticism the military government was attracting, and anticipating a rapid decline in personnel as demobilization swept the American forces out of

Europe after the Japanese surrender, Clay announced on October 5 that within two months military government would begin to withdraw from the direct supervision of local government, and the primary responsibility for the zonal administration would be placed on the Germans at all levels.[14]

During the winter, the first phase of the occupation ended—somewhat inconclusively. On January 1, 1946, government control passed from the hands of the theater and army commands to Clay's Office of Military Government (OMGUS) in Berlin and its subsidiary offices of military government in the zone. It had been expected that the changeover from military government to U.S. civilian administration would take place soon afterward, but that did not happen. The State Department, the likeliest candidate for the civilian mission, had declared that it did not have the personnel or the resources for so large a job, and the military-civilian relationship remained as it had been established by President Truman in July 1945. The State Department bore the responsibility for U.S. policy-making, and the War Department carried executive responsibility in Germany. In anticipation of the shift to civilian authority, a drive to civilianize military government offices had been under way for several months, and some progress had been made by transferring officers and their jobs to the civil service. At the lower levels, military government was being substantially but not completely withdrawn. Two and three-officer liaison teams remained to observe the work of German officials.

The effects of the military government organization shifts on the Germans were oblique but nevertheless significant. In January, the Germans went to the polls to begin a series of elections that in the ensuing six months would install new governments throughout the zone. In March, military government turned the de-Nazification process over to the Germans. To the majority of military government officers and to more than a few Germans, these steps appeared dangerous abdications of responsibility on the part of occupation authorities. That the German people, who had been subjected to twelve years of Nazi indoctrination, would be able to conduct democratic government only half a year after defeat seemed highly unlikely. An effective, German-run de-Nazification program seemed to be even less of a likelihood. General Clay responded that living democracy was the way to learn it and pointed out, in any case, that he did not have the American personnel to govern and de-Nazify the Germans. If either was to be done at all, he contended, they would have to do it themselves. Clay's position was to produce positive results. U.S. occupation was the first to restore free elections and self-government to the Germans, and the record on de-Nazification in the U.S. zone, if disappointing in absolute terms, was somewhat better than in the other three zones.

For the moment, however, the election and de-Nazification measures were criticized, particularly by field military government officers, as symptoms of the most serious lapse in U.S. occupation policy: the failure to provide a reeducation program for the Germans. During the war, it had been assumed that the Germans suffered from certain political, social, and moral deficiencies which the occupation would have to correct. The Morgenthau Plan had proposed to do so by converting them into a nation of small farmers and cuckoo clock craftsmen. President Roosevelt had said they would be required to earn their way back into the fellowship of decent nations. Opinion among those who expected to take part in the occupation had generally assumed a necessity for expensive, long-term reeducation of the Germans as individuals and reorientation of their cultural institutions; but nothing of the sort was provided for in official policy. The War Department, moreover, in its concern for administrative propriety, had not been willing to interpret its mission broadly, particularly when the result was likely to engender controversy. Those who had expected to participate in a grand social experiment were disappointed. A few American libraries, some training for German journalists, several periodicals carrying information about the United States, and a mixed fare of radio news and entertainment were the principal means of reeducation. In the first winter of occupation, the military government's Information Control Division speeded the opening of moving picture houses, and the theater command sponsored youth programs but mainly to take the Germans' minds off their immediate problems and to keep the young people off the streets.

To the occupation authorities both in Washington and in Germany, economic unification superseded all other programs. As the end of the first year of occupation approached, the country remained prostrate. The money was worthless; the economy was functioning at less than a third of the 1936 level and heading downward; the daily food ration was 1,550 calories per day in February 1946 and would fall to 1,275 in April; the relief supplies alone were costing U.S. taxpayers $200,000,000 a year. No substantial recovery could be expected as long as the country remained divided, particularly not in the U.S. zone which was a deficit area in everything but population and scenery. Half a year after Potsdam nothing had been accomplished toward economic unification. Although French opposition was more overt, it had become obvious that what the French did not block the Soviet Union would. Toward the end of March 1946, the Allied Control Council in Berlin did, after long, tortuous negotiations, complete a level of industry plan for Germany, but its principal purpose (as opposed to the Soviet's sole purpose) was to create a surplus of industrial plants and equipment for reparations. Since the Soviet Union was suspected of having already stripped its zone to far below the projected level and was demanding the largest share of the reparations available from the western zones, the plan raised the horrifying prospect of a Germany even worse off unified than divided. After the Soviet Union turned down a U.S. proposal for an export-import plan for all of Germany in the first week of April, General Clay announced, on May 3, that except for two dozen plants already allocated, the United States would halt all dismantling for reparations in its zone until it knew that Germany was to be treated as an economic unit.[15]

As John Gimbel has pointed out, Clay's dismantling stop has been variously interpreted: as an anti-Morgenthau approach to a soft settlement with Germany, as an opening salvo in the Cold War, or, as Gimbel prefers, simply an effort to secure full execution of the Potsdam Agreements.[16] Although there is no reason to doubt that either General Clay or his government wanted anything beyond economic unification, the historian looking back cannot help but see Clay's announcement as the emergence of a new course in U.S. policy. During the war, it had been assumed that the one necessity was to eliminate Germany as a threat to world peace. Opinion differed on the method but not the objective. In essence, Americans saw postwar Europe as bound to revert to the order established by the Paris Peace Conference of 1919, provided the mistakes that had been made there with regard to Germany could be corrected— no insuperable task, since everybody outside Germany had long agreed on what they were. Concentrating on restoration, American occupation policy—and military strategy as well—had not concerned itself with the possibility of the war's creating a wholly new order. If the right things were done about Germany and the proper agreements made at Potsdam, everything should settle into place easily.

Having gone to considerable effort and expense to resolve Europe's old problems for the second time in a generation, the United States did not willingly contemplate new problems. But there were new ones in 1945 and 1946. The settlement was not going to be on the terms for which the war had ostensibly been fought. Eisenhower had begun to see that at his first meeting with Marshal Georgi K. Zhukov in Berlin on June 5, 1945. Zhukov had refused to let the quadripartite control organizations start work in Berlin, and in his report to the War Department,

Eisenhower had suggested preparing for the contingency that the Control Council would be "in no sense an overall government for Germany" by being ready to administer the U.S. zone independently or administering the three western zones as a unit.[17] Truman saw it at Potsdam, and he told McCloy he would not allow the United States to be put into the position of financing reparations for the Soviet Union.[18] But the alternatives were hardly more attractive, and up to the time of the dismantling stop, in fact for a long while after, the preferred U.S. objectives remained what they had been during the war. Once the first step had been taken, however, the new course generated policy momentum of its own.

A divide had been crossed. The United States was committed to economic reunification in Germany, and to achieve it was prepared to act in new contexts. In May, 1946, at the Paris meeting of the Council of Foreign Ministers, Secretary of State James F. Byrnes offered a 25-year treaty to guarantee demilitarization and disarmament in a unified Germany. Two months later he declared the United States' readiness to merge its zone with any or all of the others. In September, speaking to the *Laenderrat* (Minister-Presidents' Council) for the U.S. zone in Stuttgart, Byrnes reiterated the U.S. desire to secure complete or partial economic unification. The tone of the speech was austere, and it left no doubt that the United States was still determined to see Germany removed as a future threat to world peace. But it also left no doubt that the other side of U.S. policy now was to see Germany rebuilt, restored to economic self-sufficiency, and allowed to govern itself. "The American people," Byrnes concluded, "want to help the German people to win their way back to an honorable place among the free and peace-loving nations of the world."[19]

The word "help" was significant. It had not occurred often in previous statements to or about the Germans. For the time being, it was still just a word. Germany was entering into the worst of the postwar winters. Life was probably harsher than it had been during either world war or during any interim years. Any existing commodities were available only for barter. American help could do no more than keep the country from barely starving. Byrnes' call for economic unification had been ignored by France and rejected by the Soviet Union. The British and U.S. zones were combined on January 1, 1947 and given the name Bizonia, but to both governments, Bizonia was a reluctant second choice for which they did not want to risk compromising whatever chances remained of getting a full economic unification. As a result, the outlay of American money increased without benefiting the Germans in either zone.

U.S. OCCUPATION POLICY IN GERMANY

By the spring of 1947, when the Council of Foreign Ministers held its fourth session in Moscow, all of Western Europe, Germany of course included, was in an accelerating downward economic spiral. The war was not, as had been hoped, a passing trauma. The continent did not have the strength to get back on its own feet. During the session, if he had not already done so beforehand, the new U.S. Secretary of State General George C. Marshall apparently concluded that this situation exactly suited the Soviet Union. While at the end of the session he expressed the opinion that progress toward a general settlement might still be made, he had by then also concluded that the prospect was not one for which it was worthwhile to prolong Europe's agony. His final report included this famous and eloquent diagnosis: "The patient is sinking while the doctors deliberate. So I believe that action cannot await compromise through exhaustion."[20]

At the Harvard University commencement on June 5, 1947, General Marshall made "in a friendly spirit" certain proposals for European recovery that quickly became known as the Marshall Plan. Although Marshall's proposals were made to the European governments—and Germany, who did not have a government, was thereby excluded—his intent from the outset was obviously to incorporate Germany in the European program. On July 11, JCS 1779 superseded JCS 1067 as the directive for the U.S. Military Governor in Germany. The new directive reaffirmed some missions given to the Military Governor in JCS 1067 and charged him with others—most of which circumstances had already forced him to assume. Chief among the latter was the effort to promote German economic unification and popular self-government. On the whole, JCS 1779 was less a new departure than a recapitulation of U.S. policy on Germany, except in two respects. First, it made "a stable and productive Germany" a principal object of U.S. policy. Second, it singled out the creation of a German central government as "a most constructive development."[21] The two together implied the inclusion of Germany in the Marshall Plan. Later in the summer, the President's Committee on Foreign Aid (Harriman Committee) included Western Germany in its study of European economic conditions. In addition to recommending substantial aid for Germany, the report stated, "All observers have determined that Germany cannot continue to exist without some kind of German Government."[22]

The United States was not yet ready in the summer of 1947 to support a separate political structure in Western Germany, but it was prepared to pursue the bizonal economic fusion with increased vigor, and it took a dim view of the prospects for either economic or political unification at the quadripartite level. Marshall had come away from Moscow convinced that the Soviet Union was not likely to agree to an economic unification that did not allow it to syphon off German resources under the guise of reparations or to a government that was not readily susceptible to Communist seizure.[23] After Moscow, at the end of May, the U.S. and British military governments brought bizonal economic agencies together in Frankfurt and established a German Economic Council with limited legislative and executive authority in economic affairs. Up until this time, the economic agencies had been scattered in various locations in the two zones. A revised level of industry announced in August raised the bizonal allotment about one-third above the four-power level set in March 1946 and reduced the amounts available for dismantling and reparations proportionally. By the time the Council of Foreign Ministers met in London in late November 1947, the United States was well past the point of waiting for compromise through exhaustion. After three weeks of meetings, in which most of the Soviet speeches were obviously addressed to an audience outside the Council, Marshall suggested that the session adjourn, which it did without setting a date for another session. The Potsdam era had ended.

For Marshall and the United States, the London session was decisive in one respect, namely, it demonstrated beyond doubt that the recovery of Europe would have to precede an East-West settlement, because the Soviet Union was banking on the opposite. In February 1948, the British and U.S. military governors moved toward establishing a government for Bizonia. Later in the month, when the six-power conference (U.S., U.K., France, and the Benelux Countries) met in London, the U.S. advocated an economically and politically unified Western Germany. By early March, when the conference adjourned temporarily, France, long the holdout against any kind of German unification, had come to the point of accepting an economic merger of its zone with the other two western zones but still adamantly opposed a political union. Two events, both unanticipated, broke the deadlock. On March 10, the murder of Foreign Minister Jan Masaryk put a brutal end to Czechoslovak independence, and on the 20th the Soviet representatives walked out of the Control Council for Germany. The Masaryk affair, in particular, was a clear warning that the West could not afford to put off decisions essential to its own security any longer, and the second round of the London Conference brought agreement on June 1 to create a government for the three western zones in Germany.

From June 1948 on, the U.S. objective was to integrate a self-governing West Germany into the European Recovery Program. The first result of the London agreement on political unification, however, was the fulfillment of an even longer standing piece of U.S. policy, namely, currency reform. Clay had proposed it in the Control Council in the spring of 1946, and it had been stalled there for two years by French opposition and Soviet insistence on an arrangement for printing money that would have left the new currency open to manipulation. On June 20, 1948, currency reform in the western zones began the West German economic miracle. The step was a big and successful one, and because it was successful, it could well have slowed progress toward a West German government had the Soviet Union not reacted on June 24 by closing the land and water routes from the western zones to Berlin. With that one move, the Soviet Union managed to dramatize both the division of Germany and the need for Western cooperation.

Even so, at the London Conference the transition from agreement in principle to the reality of a German government was slow. Everyone had qualms. The United States had the fewest qualms, and the ones it had were mostly of an abstract moral nature. American public opinion found it difficult to reconcile the principles for which the war had allegedly been fought with the swift revival of German economic and political autonomy, particularly since the evidence of genuine de-Nazification and democratization was slight. The French, who never had believed in German regeneration, and the British, who did so primarily out of fiscal necessity, feared a resurgence of German power in any form. The Germans saw themselves as extras in an East-West drama and called on stage to cheer what could be the permanent division of their country. For the Europeans, especially, the compromises were not easy, and they might not have been made at all without benevolent—and determined—U.S. mediation. When the German Parliamentary Council met on September 1, 1948 to begin writing a constitution for the western zones, U.S. policy was frankly aimed at securing German economic and political revival. The earlier occupation objectives were not abandoned, but they were negotiable. In the long winter's discussions that followed, the problems centered on finding common ground between the Germans and the French. The Germans, working under the scrutiny of the military governments, were far from being free agents, but they could play on the differences among occupying powers and did manage to write a provisional constitution, the Basic Law, that, particularly on the matter of centralization, did not coincide with the U.S. views on the subject of a proper German government. On the other hand, U.S. policy also had to make some concessions to French concerns over security and German economic competition. Consequently, the Occupation Statute, drafted at the Foreign Ministers Conferences in London in the early months of 1949, placed a potentially tighter rein on the German economy than the United States would have liked.

By the time control over German domestic affairs finally passed to the Federal Republic on September 21, 1949 and civilian high commissioners replaced the military governors, U.S. policy was entering its last stage. As U.S. High Commissioner John J. McCloy assumed his post, doubts about German readiness to be released from external controls were being brushed aside in American official circles by the push for economic recovery. U.S. policy was becoming sufficiently flexible to embrace whatever would speed German recovery within reason. German rearmament was not yet policy, but with the North Atlantic Treaty Organization (NATO) in existence, it appeared from a practical point of view to make more sense than permanent German disarmament, which was policy. World War II was a memory, although an unpleasant one. The Cold War was reality. Dean Acheson, then Secretary of State, would sum it up years later in his comment on the Paris Foreign Ministers Conference of November 1949 when he wrote: "To me one conclusion seemed plain beyond doubt. Western Europe and the United States could not contain the Soviet Union and suppress Germany and Japan at the same time. Our best hope was to make these former enemies willing and strong supporters of a free-world structure."[24]

How far had U.S. policy come? Merely from retribution to expediency? Two years after the First World War ended, Col. Erwin L. Hunt returned from his tour of duty as Chief Civil Affairs Officer, Third Army, in the German Rhineland, and stated in his final report to the War Department that the objective of future occupations ought to be to make friends of former enemies.[25] Hunt's report later became the basis for the July 1940 edition of FM 27-5, the War Department field manual on military government. The officers who conducted the post-World War II occupation of Germany were brought up on FM 27-5, not on the Morgenthau Plan or even on JCS 1067. Although the December 1943 revision of the field manual—the one in force through most of the occupation—dropped the reference to making friends out of former enemies, the objectives it set for an occupation were "to minimize belligerency, obtain cooperation, and achieve favorable influence on the present and future attitude toward the United States and its allies."[26] Since it appears that in the course of the years 1945 to 1950 these objectives were attained, perhaps in looking back, it is possible to discern an underlying consistency in U.S. occupation policy.

U.S. OCCUPATION POLICY IN GERMANY

NOTES

Where file numbers are cited the following abbreviations have been used:

ASW .... Assistant Secretary of War
CCS .... Combined Chiefs of Staff
OMGUS .... Office of Military Government (U.S.)
OPD .... Operations Division, War Department General
          Staff
USFET SGS .... U.S. Forces, European Theater, Secretary of the
          General Staff

1. U.S., Senate, Committee on the Judiciary, Subcommittee to Investigate the Administration of the Internal Security Act and Other Internal Security Laws, *Morgenthau Diary* (Germany), 20 November 1944, *1*, p. 443.
2. Memo HIS (Stimson), untitled, 5 September 1944, in ASW 370.8.
3. Henry L. Stimson and McGeorge Bundy, *On Active Service in Peace and War* (New York, New York, 1948), p. 580.
4. Cable, SHAEF 68, SHAEF Forward to War Department, 23 August 1944, in OPD ABC 387, sec. 7-A.
5. Walter L. Dorn, "The Debate Over American Occupation Policy in Germany in 1944–1945," *Political Science Quarterly* 72 (1957):494.
6. Department of State, *Foreign Relations of the United States, 1944, 1*, p. 420.
7. Summary of U.S. Initial Post Defeat Policy Relating to Germany, 22 March 1945, in OPD 336 (Section V) (Cases 104–154).
8. *Morgenthau Diary* (Germany), 2, p. 1120.
9. Ibid., p. 1079.
10. Ltr. Clay to Hilldring, 7 May 1945, in OMGUS 177-1/3.
11. Ltr. Hilldring to Clay, 21 May 1945, in OMGUS 177-1/3.
12. CCAC 69/5 (CCS 551), Directive for Military Government in Germany Prior to Defeat or Surrender, 28 April 1944, in CCS 383.21 (2–22–44), sec. 1.
13. Cable, CCS to SHAEF Main, 6 October 1944, in ASW 370.8.
14. Hqs., USFET, to CG's, Eastern and Western Military Districts, sub: Reorganization of Military Government Control Channels, 5 October 1945, in USFET SGS 041.1.
15. John H. Backer, *Priming the German Economy* (Durham, N.C., 1971), p. 111.
16. John Gimbel, *The American Occupation of Germany: Politics and the Military, 1945–1949* (Stanford, 1968), pp. 157–61.
17. Daily notes, Allied Declaration on German Defeat, 6 June 1945, in OPD, ABC 387, sec. 1-D.
18. War Diary, U.S. Cp CC, 1 W and DP Div, 1 August 1945, in OMGUS 314.81.

19. Department of State, *Germany, 1947–1949: The Story in Documents* (Washington, D.C., 1950), pp. 3–8.
20. U.S., Senate, Committee on Foreign Relations, *Documents on Germany, 1944–1950* (Washington, D.C., 1959), p. 50.
21. Department of State, *Bulletin 17*, no. 437 (November 1947):936–41.
22. *Documents on Germany*, p. 40.
23. Ibid., p. 55.
24. Dean Acheson, *Present at the Creation* (New York, 1969), p. 338.
25. Col. Irwin L. Hunt, *American Military Government of Occupied Germany, 1918–1920* (Washington, D.C., 1942), p. 88.
26. War Department, *Army-Navy Manual of Military Government and Civil Affairs*, FM 27-5 (Washington, D.C., 1943).

3

Soviet Occupation Policy Toward Germany, 1945–1949

*Barbara Ann Chotiner and
John W. Atwell*

Hollins College

Victory over Germany in 1945 confronted the Soviet Union with the greatest set of opportunities and risks since 1917. Germany was defenseless, and its formidable technological and human resources were available for exploitation. It would be up to the Soviet government to secure a maximum share of that booty. Almost all of the rest of Europe was in no condition to resist the advance of Communism, and Germany's weakness would compound that helplessness by delaying recovery. This combination of circumstances could contribute to the expansion of Soviet influence and might ultimately lead to the establishment of Communist governments throughout Europe.

By far the most serious risk lay in the possibility of a conflict with the Western Allies who could not be assumed to accept Soviet hegemony over a continent just cleared of Nazi domination. The relationship between the Soviet Union and its co-belligerents had been problematic from the outset. The wartime alliance had been founded on expediency and not on a resolution of old suspicions and fears. The rocky course of wartime collaboration portended worse to come once peace had returned, and if the point of violent confrontation was actually approached, it could find the Soviets at a prohibitive disadvantage. Behind their conquering armies stood an exhausted nation and a prostrate economy. A new war would surely result in the material collapse which had only barely been avoided in 1942. It might also find the Soviet people far less ready than before to sacrifice for the survival of a regime which millions despised. The basic principle of Soviet occupation policy in Germany was therefore a simple one: to gain as much as possible with a minimum of risk. This could be achieved only by subtlety and patience, and it required a variety of faces and techniques: camaraderie and an apparent willingness to compromise on the one hand, impatience, feigned anger, and even the threat of war on the other.

After Soviet victory at the Battle of Kursk had marked a decisive turning point in Soviet efforts to defeat the Nazis, policy-makers in Moscow began to concern themselves with Germany's future role in a postwar international system and with that state's possible relationship to the USSR. During the summer of 1943, Stalin confided to Marshall Zhukov his fears that the Western powers would try to gain full control over a defeated Germany.[1] Yet, at about the same time, Stalin also seems to have approved the formation of the National Committee for a Free Germany. Under the guidance of German Communists resident in the USSR, this organization of German prisoners of war published appeals that their countrymen overthrow Hitler, surrender to the Allies, and seek to develop a cordial relationship with the Soviet Union. Page proofs for one of the August issues of the Committee's newspaper described the group as "the nucleus of the new German regime of the future."[2] Establishment of the Free Germany Committee may very well have represented an effort to prevent the United States and Great Britain from directing German affairs after the conclusion of the war—and thus from occupying a potentially preponderant position in the new European power system. Moreover, the Committee's creation should probably be seen as an early enunciation of Soviet maximum aims with regard to postwar Germany—control over its domestic and foreign policy.

Such concerns no doubt continued to animate Stalin, his Foreign Minister V. M. Molotov, and other members of the Soviet delegation to the Yalta Conference of February 1945. Discussions at this series of meetings were intended to guide Allied military efforts during the closing months of World War II and to lay the foundations for peacetime cooperation among major powers having different socio-political systems and differing concepts of the ideal international environment. If wide-ranging cooperation among the United States, Great Britain, and the Soviet Union was to be realized, the three powers would have to be able to collaborate in administering Germany. They would have to ensure that the German economy, society, and polity would not provide the basis for a foreign policy inimical to their respective interests. In addition, Germany's joint administration could be used as a means of reducing capability imbalances among the United States, Great Britain, and the Soviet Union, so that disparities in the power positions of these states would not encourage conflict among them.

Agreements reached at Yalta seemed designed to address these points, but the undertakings also provided opportunities for the Soviets to try to use German administration to tip the European power balance in their favor. Laying the groundwork for multi-power German occupation was the reaffirmation that the wartime Allies would accept only unconditional surrender by authorized German representatives and that certain consequences would automatically flow from the capitulation. These consequences included the dissolution of the German armed forces, the abolition of the National Socialist Party and of institutions established by the Nazis or grounded in their ideology, and the "Eliminat[ion] or control [of] all German industry that could be used for military production."[3] Disarmament, along with the reduction of industrial capacity and production, would deprive Germany of the most effective means for extracting concessions from other states, and these post-surrender policies would decrease the number of states capable of threatening the Soviet Union. Hence, the domestic achievements of the Communist Party and the territorial integrity of the Soviet Union would be more secure than they had been in more than a decade. Since the abolition of the National Socialist Party and the institutions that it had established would have to be followed by the creation of new organizations, the transformational aim of Allied occupation policy promised to allow the Soviets the chance to establish at least some bases of a new Socialist system. Depending upon the success of Soviet attempts, a state might evolve whose foreign policy could be coordinated with that of the USSR. In this way, Soviet participation in the occupation of Germany might yield, not just security, but positive political gains.

The instruments through which these ends would be pursued would be the Control Council and the Greater Berlin *Kommandatura*, subordinate to the Council. Comprising the Council were to be the American, British, French, and Soviet commanders in chief of the occupation forces. Within each state's occupation zone, its senior military official was to exercise supreme administrative authority, but he was to be guided, on major policy issues affecting all of Germany, by Control Council decisions. His vote would count equally with those of the other zonal commanders in formulating policy determinations, but the negative vote of any one zonal commander would prevent the approval of any initiative. The Control Council would also oversee operations of a Central German Administration and the activities of the *Kommandatura*, a board of the four commanders of the Berlin occupation zones, which was to ensure that all sectors of the metropolitan area were treated relatively uniformly.[4] Given the tasks of the Control Council and the *Kommandatura*, the representatives of each of the four occupying powers could try to influence the evolution of German domestic politics, economics, and society in a manner consonant with policy-makers' beliefs. Were such a course to be frustrated on a national level, many similar policies could probably be carried out in a single occupation zone. In this way, even if all of postwar Germany could not play the role envisaged for it, part of the country could.

A final issue discussed at Yalta was reparations. Soviet delegates to the Conference proposed three kinds of compensation for war damages inflicted by Germany: restitution was to be made by the removal of factories and transportation means from Germany, deliveries from current German production over a ten-year period, and forced labor by German citizens. German reparations were to total twenty billion dollars, with half of the amount being received by the Soviet Union.[5] Under such an arrangement, the Soviets should have been able to reconstruct damaged industries and transportation networks quickly, thus placing their state's capabilities in a position of greater parity with those of Great Britain and the United States. While President Roosevelt and other members of the American delegation to the Yalta Conference tended to consider the Soviet proposals reasonable, Churchill and other British representatives feared that reparations on such a scale would require at least some of the occupying powers to subsidize the operation of the German domestic economy. Therefore, the conferees did not establish a firm total figure for German reparations at Yalta. Rather, Roosevelt, Churchill, and Stalin agreed that the twenty-billion-dollar figure, suggested by the Soviets, should be used as a "basis of discussion" by a lower-level reparations committee. This group was to thrash out the restitution issues in greater technical detail.[6]

Although the Yalta agreements on Germany seemed to have created a framework within which the Great Powers could cooperate, Soviet commentators soon served notice that their government did not necessarily expect such collaboration to continue after the war. Writing in the authoritative journal *Bol'shevik*, P. Chuvikov reenunciated the doctrine that war would continue to pose a danger as long as Communist and non-Communist states existed within the same international system. He also urged upon his readers the necessity of being prepared to foil new capitalist aggressions after the conclusion of World War II.[7] Given the renewed stress upon the domestic socio-economic bases of international conflict, Stalin's April 1945 remarks about Soviet occupation policy in Europe would seem to have particular significance: at a private dinner with Soviet Politburo members and a delegation of high-ranking Yugoslav Communists, Stalin told his companions that "whoever occupies a territory, also imposes upon it his social system."[8] Stalin seemed to be suggesting that—at least in the Soviet zone of Germany—the anti-Nazi transformation of society and politics would be in the direction of Soviet models. Moreover, the General Secretary probably expected these efforts at Socialist-oriented change to be attended by conflict, so that he and other Politburo associates may not have been certain that Soviet aims would be realized.[9]

Other Stalinist expressions, before the Potsdam Conference of July 1945, help to support this interpretation of Soviet aims and to extend the analysis further. The appointment of Marshall G. K. Zhukov as commander of Soviet occupation forces in Germany in late May 1945 seems to support the view that inter-Allied contention was expected. Stalin noted that decisions of the Control Council could only be taken unanimously. Therefore, said the General Secretary, Zhukov would probably need to "act alone against the other three" Council members, when its members were trying to settle various all-German problems.[10] Somewhat earlier, in his speech celebrating the Allied victory over Germany, Stalin had proclaimed the Soviet desire not to dismember that state.[11] The two sets of remarks suggest that—at the very least—Marshall Zhukov's vetoes on the Control Council would be cast when Britain, France, and the United States wished to implement anti-Nazi or reconstructive measures throughout Germany that would impede a Socialist transformation of the Soviet occupation area. The Soviets certainly could not desire the continued existence of a major central European state hostile to them. Stalin may have hoped that a Soviet representative's presence on the Control Council might provide a means of constraining the Western powers to approve policies leading to the eventual Sovietization of all of Germany. Perhaps, therefore, Stalin's disavowal of Soviet interest in the creation of several German states may be seen as an early eludication of the Soviets' maximum goals for their occupation period.

Having identified USSR aims and some costs that might be involved in pursuing them, the Soviet delegation to the Potsdam Conference negotiated the final guidelines for four-power German occupation. These arrangements defined specific steps that the American, British, French, and Soviet military governments were to take together to alter German political culture, institutions, and economic structure. Also, the Potsdam Agreements settled procedures for extracting reparations and the repayment levels that were to be made to the victors of World War II. The future of Germany—as one entity within the international system—also must have been decided. Taken together, the various clauses of the Potsdam Protocol furnished guarantees that the Soviets would be able to control their own occupation zone for their own purposes. Yet, the treaty provisions also provided opportunities for extending Soviet influence throughout the entire German territory.

With regard to the transformation of German behavior and organizations, the Potsdam Accords reiterated the Allies' intentions of preventing a resurgence of National Socialism. The Allies again undertook to abolish all Nazi political institutions—the party, the courts, the bureaucracy, the army, all deliberative bodies—and to prohibit Nazis from holding any public or major private office. While German war criminals were to be tried and penalized, laws enacted by Hitler's regime—and providing for differential treatment of various population classes on the basis of National Socialist ideological precepts—were to be abrogated. To change popular attitudes, the educational system was to be reorganized and the courses of study to be revised. To begin reviving and strengthening German democracy, non-Nazi political parties were to be allowed to establish themselves and to seek adherents. Trade unions were to be encouraged, and the freedoms of speech, press, and religion were to be guaranteed as long as they did not infringe upon the ability of the occupying powers to mold Germany's future. Whereas local governmental bodies were to be quickly reestablished to encourage mass acquisition of the habits of democratic participation, the establishment of a non-Nazi central German government was to be postponed. Presumably, the reconstitution of national law-making bodies would have to await a determination by the four major powers that a central policy-making authority would not start another military conflict. However, central German bureaucratic departments could be established to aid the Allies in transforming Germany and in exacting reparations from it.[12]

Because the Potsdam Agreements reaffirmed the principle that the commander in chief of a state's occupation forces was to be the final arbiter on all questions affecting his zone,[13] the four-power efforts to de-Nazify Germany could be interpreted by the Soviet military governor to justify a variety of measures. French, British, and American members of the Control Council might believe that these interpretations were too narrow and unduly advantaged Communist groups within the Soviet zone. However, the representatives of the Western powers could not force their Soviet counterpart to take their views into account, and the Socialist reorganization of political and cultural life in East Germany could continue. Somewhat in contrast, the Potsdam Protocol's reassertion of the Control Council's role as an agency for making all-German policy on major issues[14] would permit the Soviet military governor to urge the application of measures throughout Germany that imitated previous practice in the USSR. Should the Western powers continue to value compromise in relations with the USSR or to see agreement on German questions as an earnest of reasonably harmonious international relations, Western representatives on the Control Council might acquiesce in Soviet suggestions. Moreover, Control Council supervision over the activities of the central German authorities[15] might afford the Soviet commander opportunities to give direct orders to the bureaucrats and thus mold implementation of Council directives to benefit Soviet interests.

Questions of economic restructuring were closely tied to arrangements for reparations extraction. While the German economy was to be managed as a single entity, German citizens were not to enjoy a standard of living higher than the average experienced by other Europeans who did not live in Great Britain or the Soviet Union. Restitution payments could only be made after the means for providing the Germans with daily necessities had been secured. To ensure further that some powers would not be purchasing the necessities from their national treasuries—while others gained reparations—the Potsdam conferees agreed to several additional provisos: payments for damages inflicted during the war should come from existing plants and equipment in Germany and from labor service by Germans in the USSR. Existing stocks of goods and commodities manufactured in future years would not be earmarked for restitution but would be used to fill German domestic needs. Factories or machinery that could be used for producing armaments or for servicing armed forces and manufacturing capacity above that needed to secure the Germans an average European living standard were available for removal as restitution. The primary repayment source for each occupying power would be removals from its own zone. Yet, because the Soviet Union had been so devastated by the Nazi invasion and occupation of its territory, the USSR was also to be compensated by shipping plants and equipment from Germany's western zone to the Soviet Union. Fifteen percent of all excess industrial capacity in the three Western powers' occupation areas would go to the Soviets in exchange for deliveries of coal, foodstuffs, and other goods; another ten percent was to be transferred to the Soviets without reciprocal obligations. Each zonal commander would judge what industrial equipment constituted excess capacity and what machinery or factories were necessary for maintaining daily life in his area.[16]

Like the arrangements for German political administration, plans for economic management seemed to offer a jurisdictional basis for the Soviets to pursue in their own zone whatever policies they wished. The treaty did not provide any mechanism for overriding a zone commander's decision as to the indispensability of a particular installation for assuring minimum levels of food, shelter, and public services in his zone. The determinations made could, of course, influence the economic structures and development strategies in a given occupation area. Thus, after several years of occupation, the economies of some or all zones might be incompatible with one another. Strictures about treating Germany as a single economic entity and provisions for the derivation of reparations for the Soviet Union from the West German occupation areas might provide valuable procedural openings for Russian insistence that the Western powers implement Soviet economic policy in their zones. Should the Allies value compromise in economic matters, their agreement to Soviet demands might result in a state-dominated productive structure and Soviet-oriented trade patterns. Acquiescence might also contribute to weakening barriers to Soviet expansion at the same time that Soviet capabilities were strengthened vis-à-vis the West.

The issue of German reparations was almost certain to be divisive, because Soviet and Allied economic needs and political interests were so widely at variance. In every meeting with Allied negotiators, the Soviets revealed their intense interest in the reparations issue.

The Soviets were concerned not only with destroying Germany's ability to wage war, but they were also determined to exact a maximum of German goods and labor for their own use. Since two-thirds of Germany's prewar industrial capacity lay outside the Soviet occupation zone, the Soviets were willing to compromise with the Allies on the reparations issue in the beginning as demonstrated in the Potsdam Conferences. This strategy must have offered the best hope for the most reparations from the other zones. For a time, the Soviet's extreme need for help in rebuilding its shattered economy diminished the importance of all other matters.

The Soviets clearly had their own reparations plan which was in operation before the discussions about reparations in the Allied Control Council had even begun. The carrying out of this plan is difficult to understand, because of the secrecy with which it was conducted and the complexity of its administration. The dismantling teams were entirely separate and independent from the SMA (Soviet Military Administration).

In fact, they sometimes carried out their orders directly against SMA orders.[17]

The main requirement in the dismantling process was speed. The Soviets started removing plants and equipment from their occupation zone as soon as the surrender took place. The first stage of the Soviet removals involved "trophy teams" (*trofeinye brigady*) which were formed at division and army levels. They were composed of untrained Red Army personnel who were destructive in their work and whose acquisitions were often shamefully wasted. This was apparently of little concern to Moscow. M. Z. Saburov, who headed the dismantling operation at this time, stated his attitude at a meeting in Neuenhagen, Germany on July 2, 1945: "If we can't ship it out, it's better to destroy it so that the Germans won't have it."[18]

The first collection plan included orders for bathtubs, pianos, and accordians. Much of the original booty was collected for the personal use of Soviet officers. General Borshchev had two railway freight cars loaded with his personal treasure.[19] Generals who were sent home during 1947–48 were allowed to ship up to ten tons of personal property.[20]

Soviet sources estimate that about one-fourth of the equipment that was dismantled was actually delivered to the Soviet Union.[21] Materials were poorly packed, there were few machines to load heavy industrial equipment, and there was also a shortage of broad-gauge rolling stock. It was reported that some of the dismantled equipment lay out-of-doors for several years. Dismantling teams usually burned all of the papers that they found, including blueprints. Therefore, even if industrial equipment did eventually reach the Soviet Union, it was extremely difficult to reassemble it properly.

The first industries affected were those that produced heavy machinery, ferrous metals, and vehicles. Others included the plywood industry and hydrogen processing plants.[22] A considerable proportion of the consumer goods industry was also affected.

The total value of plants dismantled in the Soviet zone was about 1.6 billion dollars (prewar value). Up to June 1948, 1,225 plants were totally or partially taken away.[23] Six thousand kilometers of railroad track were removed and about 1,200 out of 5,500 locomotives.[24] The SMA also requisitioned 1,000 locomotives for its use.[25] By the end of 1947, nearly $600,000,000 (prewar value) of raw timber was taken.[26]

The entire Soviet occupation army was provisioned from German supplies. In addition, large amounts of foodstocks, in particular cattle and sugar, were sent to the Soviet Union. Only about one-third of the animals collected were actually delivered to the Soviet Union, because of the lack of shipping and feeding preparations. The animals collected sometimes went without feed or water for three or four days, so that most of them died en route.[27]

The Soviets had conducted a labor survey early in the occupation, and it was a simple matter to locate and draft the specialists that they needed. Most were sent to the Soviet Union. In one sweep in the fall of 1947, 10,000 workers were deported.[28]

Shortly before the end of the war, the Soviets learned of the existence of uranium deposits in southern Saxony. Inspection of the area commenced immediately after the war was over, and full-scale mining operations began in late 1947. The corporation formed to exploit German uranium was called *Vismut*. NKVD Chief Beria was the Politburo official in charge of mining operations. His assistant, Colonel General I. A. Serov, supervised on the spot. A voluntary labor campaign for *Vismut* was first attempted, but when this was unsuccessful, it was necessary to draft workers.[29]

Soviet defectors during the early 1950s provided information about a dispute over occupation policy at the highest levels of the Soviet government. According to this information, Central Committee Secretary G. M. Malenkov headed one group formed in 1944 that wished to carry out a policy of "economic disarmament" which would have dismantled much of Germany's industry and transferred it to the Soviet Union. Opposing the Malenkov group was another headed by A. I. Mikoyan, the Minister for Foreign Trade, and including A. A. Zhdanov, the Leningrad party boss; L. Z. Mekhlis, the head of the Soviet Army Main Administration for Political Affairs; and N. A. Voznesenskii, Chairman of the State Planning Commission, who fell from power and disappeared in 1949. He was replaced as Chairman of the State Planning Commission by Malenkov's protégé, M. Z. Saburov, who had directed the dismantling operation in Germany in 1945. Since there was a sharp change in the dismantling policy in 1947, there is a strong possibility that there was a major dispute over occupation policy in the Soviet Politburo.

The plan backed by Mikoyan and his group emphasized building up the economy of East Germany and concentrating on industrial deliveries rather than plant removals in order to meet Soviet needs. This led to the restoration of coal mining equipment, sugar and food processing plants, and the chemical industry.[30] Malenkov had apparently been concerned about the danger of leaving heavy industry in Germany. Mikoyan agreed that this could be dangerous but insisted that the urgent needs of the Soviet Union required that the risk be taken. The need to control these industries gave birth to the Soviet-owned German factories or SAGs. There were 134 SAGs which were the former property of the Nazi Party and other illegal organizations. The control organization for the SAGs, like that for reparations, took its orders from Moscow and not from the SMA.[31] To finance the operations of the SAG firms, two industrial and commercial banks were set up whose assets had been seized from the *Reichsbank*. The labor force of the SAGs numbered about 300,000, and the share capital was about one billion dollars (prewar value).[32]

From the German point of view, the creation of the SAGs was preferable to plant removal, because it provided jobs for German workers. Nevertheless, SAG deliveries to the Soviet Union cost the German economy about 550 million dollars (prewar value).[33] Up to 1949, the total value of forced deliveries from all industrial production was about 2.5 billion dollars (prewar value).[34]

The Soviets took the first steps toward replacing the political and economic arrangements under Nazi rule before the German surrender of May 8, 1945. These early steps must have been conditioned by the growing conviction of the Communist Party leadership in Moscow that control must, at minimum, be secured over the internal life of the USSR's occupation zone. While this belief was manifested in public and private statements made during April and May 1945—and in agreements made by the Soviet delegation at Potsdam—the attitude seems increasingly to have become the basis for administrative practice with the ascendency of Andrei Zhdanov. From at least 1945,[35] Zhdanov was the chief advocate within the Politburo of the Soviet Communist Party for a German policy that would emphasize the possibilities of turning part or all of the former enemy state into a "people's democracy."[36] Zhdanov also tended to denigrate chances of long-term cooperation between Communist and non-Communist states, while evaluating optimistically the probabilities of cooperation among states claiming adherence to Marxism-Leninism. Consequently, he stressed the importance of building Socialist institutions and engendering Soviet-type behavior patterns in Germany, so that the USSR could acquire another ally against the Western powers there.[37]

Zhdanov was in an excellent position to ensure implementation of his views by the German occupation authorities for several reasons. Malenkov—who did not believe that the Western powers would countenance the Communization of all or part of Germany—began to lose influence within Communist Party councils after mid-1945;[38] by mid-1946 he was no longer a member of the Party Secretariat.[39] Moreover, from the beginning of the Soviet occupation, Zhdanov seemed to enjoy a preponderant influence within the Soviet Military Adminstration in Germany.[40] Hence, Zhdanov was likely to have had a major voice in the formulation of policy on German occupation and the ability to secure its implementation in accord with his views. By the time that Zhdanov died on August 31, 1948, the foundations of Socialism in East Germany had, for the most part, been laid.

Attempts to alter the political life of the Soviet occupation zone—so that it began to be modelled upon that of the USSR—seem to have been two-pronged: on the one hand, Soviet occupation authorities and the German Communist Party (KPD), which they supported, worked gradually to narrow the opportunities for political choice available to the populace and to assure the implementation of decisions made by Soviet and German Communist functionaries. On the other hand, the Soviet military government sponsored a series of measures to deprive some segments of the population of the social and/or economic resources for maintaining a non-Communist orientation, while offering economic inducements to other citizens to align themselves with the Communists. Such efforts were particularly notable in the fields of political party organization and activity, the staffing and operation of governmental agencies, the nationalization of industry, and land reform. De-Nazification procedures were sometimes also used to serve the same ends.

In the first sphere of occupational activity, the Soviet military government authorized the formation of "anti-fascist, democratic" parties on June 10, 1945, although representatives of the United States, Britain, France, and the USSR had not agreed upon the guidelines to be followed for reviving widespread participation in German political life. However, the impact of this unilateral permission was severely restricted only two days later, when influential KPD member Karl Maron issued a decree in his capacity as First Deputy Lord Mayor of Berlin. Maron noted that small and/or new parties would not be allowed to organize, seek new members, or popularize a platform.[41] By restricting the number of political organizations, such a regulation would facilitate controlling party activities. Moreover, Maron's decree represents an early effort by an official receiving Soviet directives to extend regulations favoring Communist control to zones under the jurisdiction of the Western Allies.

Walter Ulbricht began reorganizing the Communist Party within Germany in May 1945. The KPD enjoyed disproportionate Soviet assistance in procuring newsprint, transportation, and financing, so that the German Communists found it easier than the Social Democrats (SPD), Christian Democrats (CDU), and the Liberals to meet the electors, publicize party programs, and develop intrazonal unity of action among local party bodies.[42] Consequently, Ulbricht's suggestion that the four parties active in the Soviet zone form an anti-Fascist bloc was meant to capitalize upon the Soviet support that his organization enjoyed and to bring it to bear upon regularized interparty bargaining. Once this popular front was created on July 14, 1945, the Socialist, Liberal and Christian Democratic Parties would not only be subject to pressure exerted directly by the Soviet military administration[43] but would have to dicker continuously with the German Communists about setting common objectives.

Having broadly circumscribed the area for distinctive party activity, the German Communists, with the support of the SMA, worked toward an amalgamation of the Social Democratic Party with the Communists. When the Social Democrats had initially proposed union with the KPD in April and May 1945, the Communists had refused the invitation. Ulbricht explained to a group of party activists that KPD members' ideological consciousnesses would first have to be better developed.[44] By early 1946, approximately 700,000 persons were affiliated with the Social Democratic Party, while between 500,000 and 600,000 had associated themselves with the KPD.

Having reindoctrinated old KPD members, educated new ones, and elaborated the chains of party command, the top German leadership proposed not just collaboration but full unification of the Socialist and Communist Parties. Numerous Socialist officials objected to this initiative, citing the appointment of Communists to administrative posts in numbers out of proportion to their party's membership strength and the tendency of Communists to present programs for approval—without discussion— at interparty meetings.[45] The Socialist functionaries seemed to be indicating fears that unification would simply work toward the massing of additional sections of the electorate behind choices made by the Communist leadership. To overcome the Socialists' resistance, political officers of the SMA met with their officers as did members of the zonal and provincial KPD elites. Intimidation by some KPD members—who were also policemen—was employed to convince individual Socialists to abandon their objections to the merger. The amalgamation was effected by the creation of the Socialist Unity Party (SED) in April 1946. In the only areas where a referendum of all Socialist Party members was held— namely the western sectors of Berlin—a majority of those voting declared themselves against the unification of the Socialist and Communist Parties.[46]

This closure of options had concrete results, both on the electoral and the intraparty levels: when elections for the provincial diets in the Soviet zone were held in October 1946, the SED received pluralities of the votes cast in all five provinces but fell short of an absolute majority in all of these jurisdictions. However, in Berlin—where the Social Democratic Party still existed in the western sectors and thus was able to run in citywide elections—the outcome of the balloting was quite different. The Social Democrats gained 63 seats, the Christian Democrats secured 29 seats, and the SED secured only 26.[47] These figures suggest that SED vote totals in the provincial elections might not have been so high, had not at least some of the electors felt that they were voting for SPD candidates and programs. Had the Soviets succeeded in persuading the British, French, and American authorities to agree upon a four-power policy with respect to political parties,[48] the SED might have run candidates in elections throughout Germany while the SPD might have been barred from fielding any. Under such circumstances, a party dominated by the Communists might have had a very important role in law-making and administration throughout Germany, and realization of Soviet maximum objectives for Germany might have been somewhat closer. On the intraparty level, the establishment of the SED was followed in 1948 and 1949 by the purging of those members who had formerly been Social Democrats and by the creation of Soviet-type structures for internal administration.[49] Thus, the number of individuals prepared to support a variety of policy alternatives was pared, and the Moscow-trained leadership around Ulbricht and Pieck acquired the machinery for forcing their views upon recalcitrant SED members.

Shifting focus from the constriction of political choice to the implementation of decisions, the Soviets and the German Communists took two kinds of steps to assure that their programs were carried out. One measure involved the placement of Communist party members in key administrative positions which provided their incumbents with the greatest leverage in influencing the course of administrative activity. Later, non-Communist incumbents of other bureaucratic posts were gradually replaced by SED members. The second group of actions comprised the creation or alteration of a whole series of governmental institutions by which centralized control could be exerted over social and economic processes occurring throughout East Germany.

After the Ulbricht and Ackermann Groups of KPD officials arrived in Germany from the USSR in May 1945, they immediately began nominating officials for appointments to governmental jobs. While the principle of appointing persons with diverse political backgrounds to every collegial administrative body was followed from the beginning, Communists tended to be named to posts overseeing public education, the police, and routine personnel selection.[50]

In the Central Administrations for the Soviet Zone, the presidents of the Bureaus for Agriculture, Education, and Finance were all Communists; all of the remaining departments—other than the Administration of Statistics—had a KPD member as vice-president. When these officials were named, between July and October 1945, the Soviets must have hoped that they might become the nucleus of a future all-German administration.[51] To the extent that the Soviets were truly sanguine about such prospects, the filling of jobs in the Central Administrations represents USSR intention to guide policy implementation throughout all four occupation areas. This aim may have lessened in importance after the formation of the SED and the subsequent exodus of non-Unity Party personnel from jobs in the Central Administrations.[52] Similar aims were displayed earlier in other settings: thus, Ulbricht urged his associates, shortly after the German surrender, to hurry in getting "reliable" individuals appointed to district governmental offices in the western sectors of Berlin. This would present the British, American, and French with *faits accomplis* and would make the governance of their own occupation zones more difficult.

Land reform and nationalization of industry deprived many Germans of economic independence. The Communists gained popular support from their expropriations. The land reform of 1945 was planned in the Soviet Union before the Nazi surrender, and the legal limit for individual landholdings became 250 hectares (about 600 acres). While fifty-one percent of the expropriated acreage was bestowed upon farm laborers or industrial workers who had not owned real property before, another thirty-two percent was bestowed upon farming families whose holdings were not large enough to make the household self-supporting.[53] Many individuals who gained advantages from these grants must have been grateful to the Soviet authorities and to the KPD, whose leaders made trips into the countryside to associate themselves with the reform.[54] Moreover, those deriving benefits from the ownership changes would be careful not to show obvious distaste for regime policies lest their land grants be revoked.[55]

The industrial reform permitting the expropriation of the property of persons identified as "war criminals and Nazi activists" was approved by referendum in Saxony on June 20, 1946. It was announced that 77.7% of the voters had approved the expropriation. The Communists had been confident of the referendum's outcome because of Saxony's radical traditions. Similar measures were promulgated by decree in the other four provinces of the Soviet occupation area. By the end of 1946, sixty percent of all industrial capital not under Soviet ownership belonged to the provincial governments of the Soviet zone.[56]

U.S. OCCUPATION IN EUROPE

The early postwar period must have been a time of great buoyancy for Soviet leaders. They had emerged victorious in the hardest fought and most destructive war in Russian history, and they controlled large parts of a Europe that was far more vulnerable to Communism than it had been in 1918. And yet the opportunities seemingly offered by their victory still eluded them. There had been almost unimaginable human and material losses within the Soviet Union, and these could not conceivably be replaced for many years. A still more significant weakness was the war-weariness of the Soviet people. These were some of the hard realities that limited the freedom of action of the Soviet leaders.

The external obstacles to Soviet ambitions were still more formidable and inhibiting. The war had brought development of a military power far greater than Germany's which was at the same time the most dangerous potential enemy that Russia had ever faced. Any foreign policy course that was chosen had to steer well clear of the terrible consequences of war with the United States.

The formulation and direction of Soviet occupation policy in Germany had to take place within the parameters set by these limitations and obstacles. The intense Soviet concentration on reparations and the soft-peddling of political interests during the early phases of the German occupation was a tacit admission of inferiority and vulnerability.

Beginning in late 1946, Soviet attitudes in the Allied Control Council and in other encounters with Allied negotiators began to harden perceptibly. This was probably a result of the conviction that the Allies were determined not to permit the exploitation of the western zones for the benefit of the Soviet Union. The policy of cooperation on reparations had produced all the returns that could be expected, and there was no longer any use for it. On the other hand, the political transformations that took place in Eastern Germany during the same period indicated a growing confidence that the Allies would not interfere with the Communization of the Soviet zone. The Berlin blockade was the clearest evidence of this new confidence. The blockade was a gamble which, if successful, would have permanently excluded Western influence from the Soviet zone. Even the failure of the blockade did not jeopardize the Soviet position in their occupation zone.

In terms of the achievement of the minimum goals in Germany defined earlier, the Soviets were undoubtedly successful. They were able to exploit Eastern Germany's resources at will, and they laid the basis for the type of political and social system suited to their own purposes. They accomplished these ends without a serious risk of war. In terms of long-range goals, the firm foothold that the Soviets had established in Germany served as an admirable platform for seizing the greater opportunities that the future would surely bring.

NOTES

1. G. K. Zhukov, *The Memoirs of Marshall Zhukov*, trans. Novosti Press Agency, Seymour Lawrence Books (New York, 1971), p. 536.
2. Wolfgang Leonard, *Child of the Revolution*, trans. C. M. Woodhouse (Chicago, 1958), p. 317; Herbert Feis, *Churchill-Roosevelt-Stalin: The War that They Waged and the Peace that They Sought* (Princeton, N.J., 1967), pp. 219–20. Descriptions of the Committee as the core of a future German government were deleted from the newspaper before the press run was begun, because the German and Soviet governments were exploring the possibility of negotiating a separate peace. Cf. Leonard, pp. 317–18.
3. Department of State, *Foreign Relations of the United States: The Conferences at Malta and Yalta, 1945* (Washington, D.C., 1955), p. 970. The precise amount of plant and equipment and the level of industrial production that marked the dividing line between Germany's possessing and lacking the capability to make war was never established at the Yalta Conference. Cf. ibid., p. 971.
4. Ibid., pp. 124–27, 956, 971.
5. Ibid., pp. 620–21.
6. Ibid., p. 983.
7. P. Chuvikov, "Uchenie Lenina-Stalina o voinakh spravedlivykh i nespravedlivykh," *Bol'shevik*, Nos. 7–8 (April 1945):25–26.
8. Milovan Djilas, *Conversations with Stalin*, trans. Michael B. Petrovich, Harvest Books (New York, 1962), p. 114.
9. This interpretation would seem to be consistent with the statements of Vladimir Rudolph, a Soviet defector who had helped to administer the removal of reparations from Germany and who had been privy to comments by several Soviet deputy ministers about deliberations within the Politburo. According to Rudolph's information, the majority of the members of the Politburo had feared, late in 1944, that the United States and Great Britain would be able to prevent the Soviet Union from turning its occupation role in Germany to its own advantage. Indeed, the Politburo members seemed to believe that the Western powers might take measures to hinder the Communization of the Soviet zone. The foremost advocate of this analysis was G. M. Malenkov. Yet, by the summer of 1945, the deputy ministers with whom Rudolph talked were claiming that Malenkov's political fortunes were declining; his Politburo colleagues no longer accepted his pessimistic predictions about the future of Soviet-Western relations over Germany. By the summer, it began to appear

that a long-term Soviet domination of East Germany would be a probable development. Robert Slusser, *Soviet Economic Policy in Postwar Germany: A Collection of Papers by Former Soviet Officials* (New York, 1953), pp. 19, 41.

10. Zhukov, pp. 657–59.
11. I. V. Stalin, "Obrashchenie tov. I.V. Stalina k narodu," *Pravda*, 10 May 1945, p. 1.
12. Department of State, *Foreign Relations of the United States Conference of Berlin* (Potsdam) (Washington, D.C., 1960), II, pp. 1481–83, 1485.
13. Ibid., *II*, 1502.
14. Ibid.
15. Ibid., *II*, 1503.
16. Ibid., *II*, 1483–87.
17. Peter Nettl, *The Eastern Zone and Soviet Policy in Germany, 1945–1950* (London, 1951), p. 62.
18. Slusser, p. 41.
19. Ibid., p. 11.
20. Ibid., p. 13.
21. Ibid., p. 15.
22. Nettl, p. 204.
23. Peter Nettl, "German Reparations in the Soviet Empire," *Foreign Affairs* 30 (1951):301.
24. Ibid., p. 303.
25. Nettl, *The Eastern Zone*, p. 217.
26. Nettl, "German Reparations in the Soviet Empire," p. 302.
27. Slusser, p. 8.
28. Nettl, "German Reparations in the Soviet Empire," p. 306.
29. Slusser, p. 132.
30. Nettl, *The Eastern Zone*, pp. 204–05.
31. Ibid., p. 63.
32. Ibid., p. 237.
33. Ibid., p. 224.
34. Nettl, "German Reparations in the Soviet Empire," p. 303.
35. Slusser, p. 41.
36. Ibid., pp. 27–28, 28n., 41.
37. Zhdanov's foreign policy views were most fully set forth in his speech on "The International Situation," delivered to the founding meeting of the Cominform at Szlarska Poreba, Poland in September 1947. The talk was published under the same title in *For a Lasting Peace, For a People's Democracy*, 10 November 1947, pp. 1–3.
38. Ibid., p. 42.
39. Robert Conquest, *Power and Policy in the USSR: The Struggle for Stalin's Succession, 1945–1960*, (New York, 1967), p. 83.
40. Slusser, p. 28n.

41. Henry Krisch, *German Politics Under Soviet Occupation* (New York, 1974), pp. 22, 57.
42. Leonard, pp. 375–76; Krisch, pp. 88, 89, 91; Nettl, *The Eastern Zone*, p. 101.
43. The SMA on occasion forced the Social Democrats and the Christian Democrats to dismiss party officials from their posts. The SMA also tried to ensure that the Social Democrats did not support unacceptable doctrines. Krisch, pp. 108–09, 117–18, 153.
44. Ibid., pp. 62–65; Leonard, pp. 425–26.
45. Krisch, pp. 92, 97, 98, 251n.
46. Ibid., pp. 121, 156–59, 163–65, 174, 183–84; Leonard, pp. 434–44. Newpapers printing statements against the unification of the Communist and Socialist Parties were, on more than one occasion, suppressed by Soviet occupation authorities.
47. Nettl, *The Eastern Zone*, pp. 90–91, 94.
48. Krisch, pp. 24–25.
49. Carola Stern, *Ulbricht: A Political Biography* (New York, 1965), pp. 111, 112; Leonard, p. 513.
50. Ulbricht's directives on the staffing of the district administration in Berlin illustrate this policy. See Leonard, p. 380.
51. Nettl, *The Eastern Zone*, pp. 114, 117.
52. Ibid., p. 116.
53. Ibid., pp. 85, 87, 182–83.
54. Stern, pp. 107–08.
55. Nettl, *The Eastern Zone*, pp. 87, 177.
56. Ibid., pp. 83, 167. See also Stern, pp. 108–09.

4

The View from USFET:
General Clay's and Washington's
Interpretation of Soviet Intentions
in Germany, 1945–1948

Jean Edward Smith
University of Toronto

Thirty-one years after the Second World War, the city of Berlin remains one of the unresolved problems of international politics. To many, it symbolizes determined resistance to Communist aggression. To others, it represents a dangerously exposed appendage of Western civilization. To still others, it looms as a jarring reminder of Nazi defeat—a city permanently divided in perpetual retribution. In the East, it appears either as a beacon of hope, or a hostile redoubt—a formidable relic of the Cold War. And in West Berlin itself, it remains a still-vigorous city—the home and workplace of two million Germans whose daily sustenance continues to depend upon quadripartite agreement of the victorious powers of World War II.

By any standard, Berlin is an anomaly. Its eastern districts (Pankow, Prenzlauerberg, Mitte, Weissensee, Friedrichshain, Lichtenberg, Treptow, Köpenick) are effectively integrated into the German Democratic Republic. Senator John Sherman Cooper presides there as U.S. Ambassador to the G.D.R.—as do his British, French, and Russian colleagues. The western sectors,[1] by contrast, remain under military occupation of the

SOVIET INTENTIONS IN GERMANY

United States, Britain, and France, a separate political entity, tied to the Federal Republic of Germany by a network of de facto arrangements but legally and constitutionally distinct.[2] Since 1948, the two sections of the city have been governed by different organs, and since August 13, 1961, East and West Berlin have been physically separated as well. Communications between the two cities have improved marginally since the border closure fifteen years ago, but the fact remains that Berlin continues to be the one point in the world where the Great Powers are in immediate, daily confrontation.

It is not the purpose of this paper to explore the contemporary Berlin situation.[3] One may argue, as Gerald Livingston has recently done, that divided Berlin provides a valuable link, joining U.S. and West German foreign policy in common purpose.[4] On the other hand, one may perhaps argue with equal justification, as both Livingston and Richard Merritt[5] at times have done, that U.S. and West German interests do not necessarily coincide in Berlin, and that rather than cementing the so-called Western alliance, the Berlin issue may arise again, as it did in 1961, as a tremendously destabilizing and, indeed, divisive factor.[6]

Rather than commenting on present conditions, this paper proposes to discuss the Berlin of the immediate postwar years. It will remind the reader that quadripartite occupation was initiated as a testament of international comity, not as a formula for discord.

In the beginning, the United States and the Soviet Union got on extremely well in Berlin. The French (and to some extent the British), not the Russians, placed the first impediments in the path of Allied cooperation, and in 1947 the United States, not the Soviet Union, abrogated the Potsdam Protocol by terminating the quarterly meetings of Foreign Ministers—an important (and often overlooked) benchmark in charting Germany's subsequent division.

It will also argue that the replacement of Secretary James F. Byrnes by General George C. Marshall accelerated the advent of the Cold War; channelled the control of U.S. policy in Germany to those who thought cooperation with the USSR was neither feasible nor desirable; contributed to the imposition of the Berlin blockade; and plunged the United States into a posture of hostile confrontation with the Soviet Union which continued for the duration of the Truman Administration.[7]

It is quite true that once the blockade was imposed, the United States (as Michael Howard has recently pointed out)[8] was in a zero-sum game with the Soviets. Their gain was our loss, and vice versa. But the mythology of the blockade and the reality of the situation as seen through contemporary eyes are two entirely different matters.

Finally, this paper will maintain that the Berlin blockade and the fever-pitched anti-Communism which it aroused in the United States contributed immeasurably to the corrosion of American public morality. As John Kenneth Galbraith once observed, the Cold War produced an American *James Bondism* "based on the thesis that Communist disrespect for international law and accepted standards of behavior could only be countered by an even more sanguinary immorality on the part of the United States."[9]

The cables which passed between Berlin and Washington and their subsequent use by the Administration reveal already in 1948 that evidence furnished by front-line participants could be juggled, tailored, and in some cases altered for ulterior political motives. If the hard evidence of Soviet belligerency was not there, it had to be manufactured, and the famous cable of March 5, 1948 sent by General Lucius D. Clay is one such example.

In conclusion, I would like to suggest several areas for additional research. General Marshall's wartime leadership has been justly acclaimed, just as has his creative sponsorship of European recovery in the non-Communist states of Western Europe. But there is a dark side to this latter accomplishment, and one which historians thus far have eschewed: namely, General Marshall's contribution to the Cold War; his reliance—celebrated by Dean Acheson, George Kennan and others—on State Department professionals (who viewed Europe in apocalyptic terms and subscribed to various demon theories of Soviet behavior); as well as his dedicated acceptance of the narrow, provincial outlook of the Administration which he so ably served.

Secretary Byrnes was not a traveled man nor was he schooled in professional diplomacy, but he shared President Roosevelt's belief that cooperation with the Soviet Union was essential if world peace was to be preserved. As Byrnes stated on his return from the Paris Peace Conference in October 1946:

> The development of a sympathetic understanding between the Soviet Union and the United States is the paramount task of statesmanship.[10]

Byrnes' closest associates in the State Department—Ben Cohen, Donald Russell, and Walter Brown—unanimously confirmed the Secretary's dedication to achieve a *modus vivendi* with the Soviet Union.[11] In Cohen's words, "compromise always appealed to Byrnes. When he could not get what he wanted, he sought an accommodation."[12] Or, as Byrnes himself phrased it:

SOVIET INTENTIONS IN GERMANY

> I know how to deal with the Russians. It's just like the United States Senate.
> You build a post office in their state and they'll build a post office in your
> state.[13]

Unfortunately, Byrnes' pragmatic attitude did not coincide with the
Cold War ideologues near President Truman, and Truman himself soon
turned on Byrnes. Fleet Admiral William Leahy (who "aspired to be
Truman's principal mentor on foreign policy"[14]), presidential adviser Sam
Rosenman, and Senator Arthur Vandenberg, in particular, saw Byrnes as a
menace and preached the inevitability of hostile confrontation with the
Soviet Union.[15]

Byrnes also encountered the unremitting opposition of State Department professionals. Part of this reflected Byrnes' preference for handling
the important issues of foreign policy personally,[16] but a more important
factor pertained to ingrained distrust of the Soviet Union bred into many
key Foreign Service members during prewar service in Baltic states
subsequently absorbed by Russia.[17] General Walter Bedell Smith, a
military officer scarcely known for his malleability, noted that the career
Foreign Service officer

> felt that the Soviet Union, owing to its peculiar structure and political
> philosophy which motivated it, was almost incapable of collaborating with
> other governments in the manner which Americans have in mind when they
> speak of collaboration.[18]

George Kennan's long cable from Moscow of February 22, 1946
describing long-range Soviet goals is a case in point.[19] It is often overlooked that Kennan's cable was sent in response to a request from H.
Freeman Matthews, Director of the Office of European Affairs, who,
together with his colleagues, had concluded that Byrnes' policy of compromise with the USSR was no longer adequate.[20] Byrnes himself was not
convinced by Kennan's pessimistic analysis and continued to believe
that an accommodation with Russia was possible. For example, when
Matthews drafted a reply for the Secretary which commended Kennan for
"a splendid piece of analysis [which] will prove most helpful to me in
considering future lines of our foreign policy," Byrnes pencilled out the
passage and substituted a simple "thanks."[21] Byrnes also objected to
circulating the cable,[22] although Matthews and Navy Secretary Forrestal
insured that it was widely read in the War and Navy Departments as
well as at State and the White House. Robert Murphy, then Political Advisor in Germany, especially congratulated Matthews. "I think you deserve
a large bouquet of orchids for having engineered this process," he wrote
Matthews on April 3.[23]

But General Clay—who shared Secretary Byrnes' dedication to seeking Soviet cooperation—was appalled by Kennan's message and even more by its circulation to military commanders. According to Murphy:

> [Clay] believes . . . that the telegram represents the British line and that it is evident that the British technique of needling our people over a period of months is bearing fruit. As you know, General Clay has regarded the responsibility entrusted to him to succeed in quadripartite government of Germany most seriously and conscientiously. An inventory of what has been accomplished in Germany he finds not too discouraging. He points out with a certain justice that while some Americans are prone and eager to blame the Soviet representatives for everything that is unhappy in the situation, an important portion of whatever blame there is clearly attaches to the French Government which thus far has done everything it could to sabotage [the Potsdam] Agreements. Clay points out, and rightly so, that apart from an active interest in reparations, restitution and intelligence matters, the French have thus far not contributed one single solitary constructive idea or effort in the entire quadripartite management of Germany.[24]

Murphy went on to remind Matthews how the British had long predicted that quadripartite government would fail and that "the only solution lay in dividing Germany, probably at the Elbe." Murphy further volunteered that the Soviet representatives in Germany could not be accused of violating the Potsdam Agreement.

> Whatever secret cynicisms they may maintain; it has not been manifest in their negotiations or official action. On the contrary, they have been meticulous in their observance of the several principles of the Potsdam Agreement . . . That their attitude toward the British and the French is permeated with distrust and suspicion, is, of course, obvious. It is also obvious that they know of British and French lack of faith in the four-power cooperation management of Germany. The fact of the matter is that there is foundation for the Soviet suspicion and distrust in this particular instance.[25]

In contrast, Murphy stated that the Soviet representatives "have gone out of their way repeatedly and throughout the months to be friendly with the Americans."

In the eyes of many Americans in Berlin, said Murphy, this reflected "a sincere [Russian] desire to be friendly with us and also a certain respect for the U.S."

> The Soviet representatives are not obtuse. They know that the American effort has made the Allied wheel go round here and that it would have stopped moving were it not for the American contribution.

Murphy also took issue with Kennan's disparagement of personal relations, for as he quite correctly told Matthews, the mutual respect between Eisenhower and Zhukov had made a definite imprint in Berlin. "Zhukov, Sokolovsky and Sobolev[26] have told me at different times and in different ways that they sincerely want the friendship of Americans, that there will never be a war between the two countries, that they are grateful for what the United States has done for the Soviet Union, but that they simply do not trust the U.K. . . ."[27]

Murphy concluded by noting that the increasing appearance of tension might aid the passage of the Administration's U.M.T. bill.

> However, I would like to make it quite clear that in our local innocence [in Berlin] we have never and still do not believe for a minute in imminent Soviet aggression.[28]

Murphy's letter (which is not printed in the *Foreign Relations of the United States*) deserves to be quoted at length, because it reveals that those closest to the Russian presence in Germany did not despair of Soviet cooperation. Clay, in particular, saw no reason for alarm. In fact, the military in Germany continued to stress the importance of Great Power harmony.

Bear in mind that it was Eisenhower and Clay who prevailed on Harry Hopkins in 1945 to expedite SHAEF's withdrawal from the Soviet zone,[29] and that Clay, who met regularly with the Russians on the Allied Control Council, had thus far (in mid-1946) not presented a single major complaint to Washington concerning Soviet belligerency.

On the contrary—in June 1945 he wrote McCloy that "with patience and understanding we will be able to work out central controls" with the Soviets. "I am just as apprehensive [Clay continued] over possible impatience and lack of understanding at home . . . as I am of our ability in the long run to work out many mutual problems of the Allied Control Council."[30]

And again, on September 3, also to McCloy, Clay wrote:

> . . . I am much encouraged by the general attitude and apparent desire, *especially on the part of the Russians*, to work with us in solving the various problems. I believe we are making real headway in breaking down their feelings of suspicion and distrust. I am hopeful that by the time conflicting views develop on major issues, we will understand and trust one another sufficiently to deal with the problems objectively *and to work out sensible compromises of our views.*[31]

In effect, Clay, who knew Byrnes intimately from his prior service as Deputy Director of War Mobilization and Reconversion, was attempting to pursue in Germany the policy the Secretary espoused. Thus, when he returned to Washington in November 1945, Clay reminded State Department officials[32] that it was the French, not the Russians, who were blocking four-power government. When Clay asked Matthews whether the U.S. was prepared to bring pressure on France, Matthews demurred. Similarly, [according to General John Hilldring's report of the meeting] Clay "took sharp issue with the point of view that it was the USSR which was failing to carry out the Berlin [Potsdam] Protocol." According to Clay, the Russians favored the creation of central administrative machinery which the French continued to veto. In fact, Clay "felt there was some merit to the Russian position that barriers to interzonal movement could only be removed after the establishment of central administrative machinery."[33] Clay also thought that the Russians "had gone further than the French in the introduction of democratic procedures in their zone"—which may be hard for some dedicated cold warriors to swallow (as it undoubtedly was for Matthews and Riddleberger). As for such Soviet action as the zonal land reform, Clay reminded his conferees that the Russians were "acting unilaterally in the absence of quadripartite agreement." But then, "so was the Commanding General, U.S. Forces, European Theatre." According to Clay:

> The entire record of the Control Council showed that the USSR was willing to cooperate with the other powers in operating Germany as a single political and economic unit. The USSR had blocked no more than one or two papers in the Control Council, which is more than can be said for the other members.[34]

Clay, therefore, brusquely rejected James Riddleberger's suggestion that reparations be used as a lever against the Soviets.

On such issues as the vesting and marshalling of German external assets,[35] restitution,[36] and reparations,[37] the fact is that U.S. military government in Germany accepted the merit of Soviet arguments, while the State Department, particularly at working levels below Secretary Byrnes, was already fashioning an Anglo-American entente which at the very least worked at cross purposes to quadripartite control.

A pertinent illustration involves the use of German patents and scientific data. On May 27, 1946, three weeks after the American cut-off of reparations deliveries, Clay protested a planned meeting of Western countries in London (organized by the State Department) to discuss German patents. The Soviet Union was to be excluded. But as Clay saw it:

> If we are to adhere to the principles of quadripartite government of Germany, advance agreements among the Western powers add to our difficulties . . . Patents belong to Germany as a whole. It would not appear that they could be made available under the Potsdam Protocol except under such conditions as would be agreed by quadripartite machinery.[38]

Similarly, when the State Department sought to establish Radio Liberty in Munich in August 1946 (broadcasting in Russian to the Soviet

Union), Clay again protested. "I cannot agree," he told Washington, "that the establishment of a broadcasting station in Germany to broadcast to the Soviet Union in the Russian language is in the spirit of quadripartite government." Again, Clay lost.[39]

It is not surprising, therefore, that when General Eisenhower, then Army Chief of Staff, queried all military commanders "on the manner in which agreements had been carried out by the Soviets,"[40] Clay replied that:

> It is difficult to find major instances of Soviet failure to carry out agreements reached in quadripartite government of Germany. Our difficulties in this field arise not so much from failure to carry out agreements but rather from failure to agree on interpretations. . . . In most such instances, French unwillingness to enter into agreements relative to governing Germany as a whole makes it difficult to place blame on Soviets.[41]

This was five months after Kennan's Cold War forecast from Moscow. But Clay's dispassionate assessment was ignored once again.

The point of this diversion is to emphasize once again that insofar as Germany was concerned, the Cold War was neither inevitable nor inherent; certainly it was not sought by those in command of U.S. military government. Indeed, the standards of political propriety then observed by America's overseas' command are illustrated by General Clay's response to advice[42] that he intervene in forthcoming Berlin elections on behalf of non-Communist parties. To Clay, such intervention was unthinkable. "If we did this," he said, "military government would have clearly violated its announced principles of political neutrality and such action . . . would prove a step backward in teaching democracy."[43]

In a refreshing glimpse of what America once stood for, Clay advised Washington that:

> We have created a reasonably healthy political atmosphere in our zone in which there is little evidence of Communist gains. It is my view that the direct support of political parties by military government would harm our political gains and would do little to retard the development of the Socialist Unity Party and its efforts in Berlin.

Clay, whose father had been a three-term United States Senator from Georgia, then put the matter into context. After all, he told Washington, the measures about which some persons "have become most excited are not too different from election measures sometimes pursued in large cities in democratic countries."[44]

The end of 1946 brought no dramatic change. The American and British zones of Germany were fused for economic purposes only,[45] and Clay remained more concerned about French intransigence than Communist competition.[46] At the governmental level, Secretary Byrnes—to the dismay of Administration hard-liners[47]—reached agreement with the Soviet Union and successfully completed the peace treaties for the former German satellites. In fact, Byrnes was guardedly optimistic for the future of U.S.-Soviet cooperation. In a speech on January 11, 1947, the Secretary stated:

> Today I am happy to say I am more confident than at any time since V.J. Day that we can achieve a just peace by cooperative effort if we persist with firmness in the right as God gives us the power to see the right.[48]

Byrnes believed the successful conclusion of the satellite treaties offered promise of a rapid peace treaty for Austria; even in the far more complicated case of Germany, he saw hope. The German discussions, he said, "will start under much more favorable circumstances than seemed possible until last month."[49] Byrnes reminded his audience that "nations, like individuals, must respect one another's differences,"[50]—a theme which characterized his diplomacy.

But Byrnes was on his way out as Secretary of State. As Robert Murphy delicately phrased it, Truman and Byrnes "lacked the mutual confidence which should prevail between the man in the White House and his chief foreign affairs adviser."[51] Accordingly, Truman had "secretly" asked General Marshall to replace Byrnes,[52] and when he learned of the shift, Byrnes promptly resigned.

American policy toward the Soviet Union changed abruptly. Unlike Byrnes, Truman appears to have abandoned hope of reaching substantive agreement with the Soviet Union,[53] and, confronted with a threatened British pull-out in the eastern Mediterranean, seized the opportunity to proclaim the Truman Doctrine—a formal declaration of a state of Cold War.[54] As Truman wrote Margaret immediately afterwards, "I knew at Potsdam that there is no difference in totalitarian or police states, call them what you will, Nazi, Fascist, Communist or Argentine Republics. . . ."

> The attempt of Lenin, Trotsky, Stalin, et al., to fool the world and the American Crackpot Association, represented by Jos. Davies, Henry Wallace, Claude Pepper and the actors and artists of immoral Greenwich Village, is just like Hitler's and Mussolini's so-called Socialist states.
>
> Your Pop had to tell the world just that in polite language.[55]

But as George Elsey (then a White House assistant) protested to Clark Clifford, "there has been no overt action in the immediate past by the USSR *which serves as an adequate pretext* for [such an] 'All-out' speech."[56] The fact is that Truman had sought to proclaim his own "get tough" policy toward the Soviet Union for some time[57] and seized on the first opportunity. Yet, by portraying Soviet-American differences as a clash of two mutually irreconcilable ideologies, Truman, Marshall, Acheson, and Clifford trapped themselves in an escalating cycle of rhetoric and response which significantly limited U.S. alternatives in dealing with Moscow.

Secretary Byrnes, by contrast, refused to accept the simplistic dichotomy postulated by his successors. He could never bring himself to endorse the "Truman Doctrine," and in his first speech after leaving office, Byrnes went out of his way to deny that conflict with the Soviet Union was inevitable. "On the contrary," Byrnes said, "I believe we can make peace and we can keep the peace. . . ." Thus, he reminded his audience:

> We have made it clear to the Soviet Union that it cannot dictate the terms of peace. We must also realize the United States cannot dictate the terms of peace.[58]

The Truman Doctrine was announced while General Marshall was in Moscow at the Conference of Foreign Ministers. Certainly, it did not improve the chances for reaching agreement with the Soviet Union [Germany was the principal issue under discussion], but it could scarcely have embarrassed Marshall, for as Dean Acheson reports, the speech Truman delivered had been approved by Marshall before his departure for Moscow.[59]

The new rigidity of American foreign policy, combined with the dismal failure of the Moscow Conference—for which the United States was scarcely blameless—caused Clay to be morose. As he wrote Walter Brown of South Carolina:

> I was, of course, shocked when Justice Byrnes resigned and am afraid I have not had the same heart for my work since. This was particularly true of Moscow, and after being there for two weeks I asked and received permission to return to my duties here in Germany.[60] Believe it or not, *I am still trying to practice the type and kind of democracy which we all believed in and with real hopes for its success if America is patient* and truly prepared to support such a program.[61]

Differences between Clay and Washington mounted in 1947 as Clay stressed the economic problems confronting Germany, while Washington appeared more concerned with fashioning an anti-Soviet alliance.[62] The issue came to a head in July when Clay asked to be replaced. "I feel that State Department wants a negative personality in Germany," he telexed Assistant Secretary of War Howard Petersen.

> As you know, I can carry out policy wholeheartedly or not at all and there is no question left in my mind but that my views relative to Germany do not

coincide with present policies. . . . Request orders calling me back for coal conference [scheduled to be held in Washington] which also authorizes shipment of personal belongings.[63]

General Eisenhower, Army Chief of Staff, and a close personal friend, intervened to remind Clay that as soldiers they could not quit "simply because things sometimes go at sixes and sevens." National policy was set in Washington, said Eisenhower, and Washington viewed the international situation as critical.[64] Clay got the message; henceforth he realized that U.S. policy in Germany would march to a different drummer. "It is true that we here cannot be aware of critical international situation if we are not kept informed," he replied to Eisenhower—a rather curious observation for the man in daily contact with the Russians. Clay said he realized "that broad policy must be set in Washington." "If you think that my departure would be running out on the job and failing in my obligation," he told Ike, "that is enough to keep me here."[65]

For more than two years, Clay had operated under the belief that his task was to achieve effective four-power government; he believed in being firm but correct with the Russians, and he still thought such a policy would succeed.[66] But Washington, it was now clear, placed a higher premium on the anti-Soviet alliance, and with it, Germany's division.

With the line of march thus charted, it is not surprising that the situation in Germany deteriorated quickly. The London Conference of Foreign Ministers, meeting in December 1947, collapsed in an impasse over Germany. Secretary Marshall terminated the session abruptly[67]— blaming Soviet obstructionism—and plunged forthwith into extensive bilateral talks with Britain pertaining to the economic and political organization of the western zones.[68]

In January 1948, the State Department moved to take over complete responsibility for German occupation. Without bothering to inform Clay beforehand, Marshall announced that State would assume control on July 1st.[69] And while the army had been advocating such an action for some time, the form of Marshall's announcement further suggests that relations between Clay and the Administration had eroded considerably since Byrnes' departure.

To succeed Clay, Marshall chose Walter Bedell Smith, then U.S. Ambassador in Moscow: a rigid man (and long-time Marshall intimate) who would doubtless give American policy in Germany the hard-line focus Washington desired—and who previously had been turned down for the German post by Secretary Stimson as temperamentally unsuitable.[70] This time it was former Secretary Byrnes who intervened (appointment as Military Governor required Senate confirmation), and the planned State

Department takeover did not occur until late 1949, following creation of the West German government, when John J. McCloy became U.S. High Commissioner.

In February, while Congress debated the Marshall Plan for European recovery, Czechoslovakia receded further behind the Iron Curtain as the non-Communist members of government were ousted. Doomsayers in Washington believed their predictions fulfilled, although as George Kennan has noted, such a move changed very little and should have been anticipated.[71]

On the heels of events in Prague, Lt. Gen. S. J. Chamberlain, Director of Army Intelligence, visited Clay in Berlin. He impressed on Clay the pitiful unreadiness of U.S. armed forces, the fact that major military appropriations were pending before Congress, and the need to galvanize public support for substantial rearmament. Accordingly, on March 5, 1948, Clay dispatched a TOP SECRET cable to Chamberlain to assist the Army chiefs in their testimony (on U.M.T.) before the Senate Armed Services Committee the following week. It read as follows:

> For many months, based on logical analysis, I have felt and held that war was unlikely for at least ten years. Within the last few weeks, I have felt a sudden change in Soviet attitudes which I cannot define but which now gives me a feeling that it may come with dramatic suddenness. I cannot support this change in my own thinking with any data or outward evidence in relationships other than to describe it as a feeling of a new tenseness in every Soviet individual with whom we have official relation. I am unable to submit any official report in the absence of supporting data but my feeling is real. You may advise the chief of staff [Bradley] of this for what it is worth if you feel it is advisable.[72]

As is now well known, this message sent shock waves through Washington. According to Walter Millis, editor of the *Forrestal Diaries*, it "fell with the force of a blockbuster bomb." Forrestal copied the cable verbatim in his diary, one major indication of the "intense alarm [it caused] among those who were aware of it."[73] Certainly, its impact was profound.[74] But the important point is that insofar as Clay was concerned, it was not triggered by any change in the Berlin situation.[75] It was tailored to fit the needs of the American military in Congressional testimony.[76] And as Michael Howard has pointed out:

> This was not to be the last occasion on which the American military were to try to influence congressional opinion by an inflated estimate of Soviet intentions and capabilities, but it may well have been the first and most significant.[77]

In fairness to Clay, it must be recognized that he did not envision how the cable would be used or what its effect would be. His intent was to assist the army before Congress; it was not to create war hysteria in the country. In fact, Clay was appalled when its contents were leaked to the *Saturday Evening Post*.[78] "The revelation of such cablegram," he advised Bradley, "is not helpful and in fact *discloses viewpoint of responsible commander out of context with many parallel reports.*[79]

Clay was anything but a political neophyte and perhaps should have anticipated what effect his March 5 message would have. On the other hand, as he himself points out, his regular command cables to Washington throughout this period stressed the improbability of the Soviet Union actually wanting war. Probably, Clay simply could not conceive that his superiors would accept the cable to Chamberlain (which after all was deliberately not sent through command channels) and ignore his calm official assessments. The fact, of course, was that those in command in Washington—Truman, Marshall, Forrestal, Lovett, perhaps Bradley, and certainly many of their minions in State, Defense, and the intelligence community,[80] firmly believed the Soviet Union was intent on war, and Clay's unofficial cable confirmed their assumptions. Indeed, precisely because of Clay's more sober analyses and because of his prior commitment to cooperating with the Soviets, the impact of the Chamberlain cable was even greater than it might have been had Clay thought otherwise. This, of course, is dependent upon the supposition that the highest echelon of the U.S. government accepted the March 5 cable as genuine: that they honestly believed it, instead of merely using it to whip up an anti-Soviet reaction. If the latter is true, then the highest leadership of the 1948 Truman Administration bears the gravest responsibility. [At present, because of declassification problems, this author is unwilling to make a judgment on this issue.]

Without detailing the events which led from the Clay telegram to the Berlin crisis of 1948–1949, this writer concludes—with George Kennan—that Soviet actions in Berlin (and Czechoslovakia) were defensive reactions to the success of the Marshall Plan and U.S.-U.K. efforts to create a separate West German government.[81] Contrary to the raft of Cold War literature about the Berlin blockade[82]—including Clay's own *Decision in Germany*—the fact is that the Soviet Union blundered into the blockade in response to a particular set of circumstances, and not, as orthodox mythology tells us, as part of a global conspiracy or master plan laid carefully in advance.

Clay, in particular, discounted Soviet intentions to go to war throughout the blockade. On June 25, he judiciously told Washington, "I do not expect armed conflict. . . . If Soviets go to war, it will not be because of Berlin currency issue [the pretext for the blockade] but only because they believe this is the right time. In such case, they would use currency issue as an excuse. *I regard this probability as rather remote. . . .*"[83]

Clay's repeated refusal to withdraw American dependents from Berlin (the Department of the Army continually pressed such a move)[84] and especially his proposal to move through to Berlin along the autobahn, reflected his long-standing appreciation that the Soviet Union genuinely did not want war. Indeed, in this context, Clay's suggestion to test the blockade with an armored column was based on a cautious, sound judgment of Soviet intent. Unlike Washington, Clay had not yet formed a preconceived opinion of Soviet expansionism. Thus, where Washington tended to see each new Soviet gambit as a step leading inexorably to hostile confrontation—and to stress continually the exposed military position of Berlin (Marshall, Bradley, and Bedell Smith were particularly guilty of this)—Clay rested his case on three years of first-hand experience in dealing with the Russians in Germany. The Soviets simply did not want war, and never did, and Clay knew it.[85]

This, I believe, explains much of the wrangling between Berlin and Washington in 1948. In Washington, the leaders of the Truman Administration were witnessing a self-fulfilling prophecy. They had based American foreign policy on the inevitability of a confrontation with the Soviet Union, and now that policy was being realized. In Berlin, by contrast, the situation appeared merely as one more round, albeit an important one, in the political contest for Germany's future.

Similarly, one must distinguish between the effects of the blockade and the "lessons" America has drawn from it. The effects, pragmatic and political, were to hasten the formation of a West German government and to provide, over the long run, two separate German states, each committed to its respective alliance, peacefully coexisting in a Europe which, for the first time in one hundred years, harboured little fear of German imperialism. This is no small blessing, and indeed, was the purpose for which the Second World War was fought in the first place.

The so-called "lessons" of the Berlin blockade, however, have been largely pernicious. Not only did they retard the detente which now exists in Germany, they also provided symbolic rationale for a host of specific policies pursued subsequently. As Gaddis Smith has pointed out, the blockade did not end when the barriers were raised in May 1949.

> It still lived on in the minds of policy-makers and still exercises its influence on the content and style of American diplomacy.[86]

The orthodox interpretation of the blockade involves a litany of American virtue and Soviet iniquity. An easy recipe for success evolved in which all Soviet actions were interpreted as a master plan of aggression requiring immediate military confrontation. The Soviets backed down in Berlin, so the lesson goes, because they were met with superior American power. And the premise that the blockade reflected a Russian global strategy rather than a local response to Western initiatives went largely unchallenged.

Berlin became the ultimate testing point—the global showdown, a test of freedom versus slavery. The analogy between Communism and Nazism, belaboured by Truman and others, permeated American thinking. Negotiations henceforth were spurned and skepticism eschewed. A pervasive righteousness encrusted U.S. policy which not only limited diplomatic flexibility but soon aligned the United States with every reactionary regime extant. Global opposition to Communism was sufficient to justify whatever excesses (foreign and domestic) policy-makers deemed necessary. The undeclared war in Korea and the tragedy of Viet Nam were in no small measure the results of this attitude. Most serious, however, was the resulting corrosion of American public morality. The honest, sincere belief in the qualitative superiority of American democracy; the human decency it once stood for in the eyes of the world; the important procedural safeguards which insured it, and the even-handed treatment of political opposition became, to some extent, an unfortunate casualty of the blockade.

NOTES

1. Comprising the districts of Reinickendorf and Wedding (France); Tiergarten, Charlottenburg, Spandau and Wilmersdorf (U.K.); and Zehlendorf, Steglitz, Schöneberg, Kreuzberg, Tempelhof and Neukölln (U.S.).
2. Although Articles 23 and 144(2) of the Basic Law include Greater Berlin as a component Land of the Federal Republic, the Western Military Governors declined to approve these provisions (see Ltr., Military Governors to Dr. Konrad Adenauer, 12 May 1949, reprinted in B. Ruhm von Oppen, *Documents on Germany Under Occupation, 1945–1954* (Oxford, 1955), pp. 390–91). This position was confirmed by the Four Powers in the Berlin Accords of 3 September 1971. Cf. Robert Gerald Livingston, "Germany Steps Up," *Foreign Policy* 22 (1976):177.
3. A useful discussion of future senarios is contained in Richard Merritt, "Divided Berlin: One Past and Three Futures", *Journal of Peace Research* 9 (1972):331–44.
4. Livingston, "Germany Steps Up", op. cit.
5. Merritt, op. cit., p. 336.
6. The early opposition of former Secretary of State Dean Acheson, John

J. McCloy, and General Clay to negotiation of the 1971 Berlin Accords, and especially to the leading role of Chancellor Brandt, is illustrative of the difficulties which can arise. See *New York Times*, 3 January 1971.

7. James Byrnes' role as Secretary of State has been misinterpreted by revisionists and traditionalists alike. For a genuine appraisal based on extensive primary research into the original documents of the period—many which have only recently become available, I am deeply indebted to John F. Karl of the University of Toronto. Karl's findings are cogently and objectively presented in "Compromise or Confrontation: James F. Byrnes and United States' Policy Toward the Soviet Union, 1945–1946" (Ph.D. diss., University of Toronto, 1975). Cf. Gar Alperovitz, *Cold War Essays* (New York, 1970), pp. 73n, 95; Barton J. Bernstein, "American Foreign Policy and the Origins of the Cold War", in Bernstein, ed., *Politics and Policies of the Truman Administration* (Chicago, 1972), pp. 23 ff., 54; Gabriel and Joyce Kolko, *The Limits of Power* (New York, 1972), pp. 42–43; Lloyd Gardner, *Architects of Illusion* (Chicago, 1970), pp. 101–03. The traditionalist view is restated in Herbert Feis, *From Trust to Terror* (New York, 1970), pp. 54–55, 58–60, 63–87.

8. Michael Howard, Governor General of Germany," *Times Literary Supplement*, 29 August 1975, p. 970. Also see Gaddis Smith, "The Berlin Blockade Through the Filter of History: Visions and Revisions of the Cold War," *New York Times Magazine*, 29 April 1973, pp. 13 ff.

9. John Kenneth Galbraith, "The Sub-Imperial Style of U.S. Foreign Policy," *Esquire* 77 (1972):79–84.

10. James F. Byrnes, "Report on the Paris Peace Conference," 18 October 1946, *Department of State Bulletin*, Vol. 15, p. 741 (18 October, 1946).

11. Interview, Ben Cohen, 20 June 1974; 18 November 1974; Donald Russell, 12 December 1974. Diary of Walter Brown, 9 September 1945, Byrnes MSS file 602 (Clemson). Also, see the Journal of Joseph E. Davies, Davies MSS, Box 18 (Library of Congress) as cited in John F. Karl, "Compromise or Confrontation," p. 46.

12. Interview, 18 November 1974, cited in Karl, op. cit., p. 6.

13. Edward Weinthal (*Newsweek*), interview, Dulles Oral History Project, Princeton University Library, 11 May 1966, p. 1.

14. John Morton Blum, ed., *The Price of Vision: The Diary of Henry A. Wallace, 1942–1946* (Boston, 1973), p. 463.

15. Vandenberg's perspective is capsuled in the following statement made to former Secretary of State Cordell Hull: "The consequences of a policy of tolerance, patience, and respect [for the Soviet Union] would lead to another Munich and its consequences." Davies Journal, 22 May 1945, Davies MSS, Box 17 (Library of Congress).

16. See, for example, Dean Acheson's scathing comment: "Byrnes oper-

ated entirely personally with a very small number of people. As far as Mr. Byrnes was concerned, the State Department consisted of about six people . . . what the rest of the Department did was no concern of his and he did not want to be bothered about it." Acheson MSS, Box 64, Transcript of "Princeton Seminar," 2 July 1953 (Truman Library). See also Charles Bohlen, *Witness to History* (New York, 1973), pp. 248, 256–59.

17. Loy Henderson and George Kennan are the best examples. See Karl, op. cit., p. 15 (citing interview with Henderson, 20 March 1975). Also, see George F. Kennan, *Memoirs, 1925–1950* (Boston, 1967), p. 24.

18. Walter Bedell Smith, *My Three Years in Moscow* (New York, 1949), p. 30.

19. Kennan to Byrnes, 22 February 1946. *Foreign Relations of the United States* 6 (1946):696–709.

20. Matthews to Kennan, 13 February 1946. Records of the Department of State, filed with 861.00.

21. Draft of Byrnes to Kennan, 27 February 1946, drafted by H. Freeman Matthews, Records of Department of State, filed with 861.00. By contrast, Matthews cabled Kennan, "I cannot overestimate its [Kennan's cable] importance to those of us here struggling with the problem." It is not clear whether Matthews was referring to the Soviet Union or Secretary Byrnes. See Matthews to Kennan, 25 February 1946, Records of the Department of State, filed with 861.00.

22. Byrnes modified his objection insofar as it might aid the pending British loan request on the Hill, but cautioned that it be handled very discreetly. See Minutes of the Committee of Three [Byrnes, Patterson, Forrestal], 28 February 1946. Records of the Department of State, filed with 811.0200.

23. Letter, Murphy to Matthews, 3 April 1946, Records of the Department of State, filed with 861.00. For the discovery of this cable, I am especially indebted to John F. Karl.

24. Ibid.

25. Ibid.

26. Arkady Alexandrovich Sobolev, Chief, Political Section, Soviet military Administration in Germany.

27. Murphy to Matthews, 3 April 1946.

28. Ibid.

29. Clay (signed Eisenhower) to Combined Chiefs of Staff, 2 June 1945; Clay (signed Eisenhower) to Joint Chiefs of Staff, 6 June 1945; Clay (signed Eisenhower) for Marshall, 8 June 1945, reprinted in Jean Edward Smith, ed., *The Papers of General Lucius D. Clay: Germany, 1945–1949*, 2 vols. (Bloomington, 1974), *1*, 16–23. See also Robert Sherwood, *Roosevelt and Hopkins: An Intimate Story* (New York, 1948), pp. 913–14.

30. Clay to McCloy, 29 June 1945, reprinted in *Clay Papers, 1*, 35–45.
31. Clay to McCloy, 3 September 1945, reprinted in ibid., pp. 62–68. Italics added.
32. William L. Clayton, Willard L. Thorp, H. Freeman Matthews, Seymour J. Rubin, James W. Riddleberger, Charles P. Kindleberger and John de Wilde. For the report of these conversations kept by General John Hilldring, see *Clay Papers, 1*, 111–17.
33. As Professor John Gimbel has pointed out repeatedly, the cut-off of reparations deliveries which Clay ordered in May 1946 was aimed primarily at the French, not the Russians—who, of course, were also affected. See Gimbel, "Cold War, German Front," *The Maryland Historian* 2 (1971):41–55; Gimbel, *The American Occupation of Germany: Politics and the Military, 1945–1949* (Stanford, 1968), pp. 59–61.
34. Hilldring minutes, *Clay Papers, 1*, 113.
35. Clay to Hilldring, 25 January 1946 [CC22138]; Clay to Hilldring, 8 February 1946 [CC22830]; Clay to Hilldring, 9 February 1946 [CC22881]; Clay to Hilldring, 17 February 1946 [CC23226]; Clay to Hilldring, 18 February 1946 [CC23277]. Reprinted in *Clay Papers, 1*, 149–51, et seq.
36. See, for example, Clay to Hilldring, 29 December 1945 [CC21041], reprinted in *Clay Papers, 1*, 140–41.
37. Clay to Hilldring, 23 November 1945 [CC19295]; Clay to Hilldring, 28 November, reprinted in *Clay Papers, 1*, 123–26.
38. Clay to Echols, 27 May 1946 [CC5824], reprinted in *Clay Papers, 1*, 223–24. Clay's protest was to no avail. For the London Accord on Treatment of German Owned Patents, 27 July 1946, see *TIAS*, No. 2415.
39. Clay to War Department, 12 August 1946 [CC1697]; also see Clay to War Department, 2 September 1946 [CC2948]. Reprinted in *Clay Papers, 1*, 249–50, 261. See Acheson to Byrnes, 21 August 1946, *Foreign Relations of the United States* 5 (1946):687–89.
40. War Department cable WX-95097 (20 July 1946). Eisenhower's cable was designed to solicit corroborating material for the bellicose memorandum on Soviet policy then under preparation by Clark Clifford and George Elsey. See Richard M. Freeland, *The Truman Doctrine and the Origins of McCarthyism* (New York, 1970), pp. 56–57. For the text of the Clifford-Elsey memorandum, see Arthur Krock, *Memoirs* (New York, 1968), pp. 419–82.
41. Clay to McNarney, 23 July 1946. Reprinted in *Clay Papers, 1*, 243–44. It was apparent to Secretary Forrestal that Clay's perception of Soviet activity differed fundamentally from his own. When Clay told Forrestal on July 16, that "the Russians did not want a war and that we should find it possible to get along with them," Forrestal thought Clay was nearing a mental breakdown. "He [Clay] runs the

risk of blowing up entirely," Forrestal wrote Stimson—a comment which probably says as much as one needs to. Walter Millis, ed., *The Forrestal Diaries*, pp. 182–83.

42. See Acheson to Murphy, 16 August 1946, and the reference cables cited therein. *Foreign Relations of the United States* 5 (1946):732–33.

43. Clay for War Department, 20 August 1946 [CC2135], reprinted in *Clay Papers*, 1, 256–58.

44. Ibid.

45. For discussions pertaining to economic fusion, see *Foreign Relations of the United States* 5 (1946):635 *ff*.

46. In particular, Clay was most concerned about French efforts to detach the Saar from Germany and ultimately appealed directly to Byrnes on the issue. See *Clay Papers*, 1, 279–93. Also see *Decision in Germany*, pp. 132–33.

47. Notably Fleet Admiral William Leahy. See Arthur Krock, "Admiral Leahy's Role," *New York Times*, 26 March 1947.

48. *Department of State Bulletin* 16, p. 88 (11 January 1947).

49. Ibid., p. 89.

50. Ibid., p. 89.

51. Robert D. Murphy, *Diplomat Among Warriors* (Garden City, New York, 1964), p. 305.

52. Ibid. Also, see Dean G. Acheson, *Present At the Creation: My Years in The State Department* (New York, 1969), p. 283.

53. See especially Arthur Krock, "In the Nation," *New York Times*, 23 March 1947, and the Ben Cohen interview cited in fn. 11, as well as interviews with two other Truman confidants, not authorized for attribution, in Karl, "Compromise or Confrontation," p. 419.

54. For text, see *Public Papers of the Presidents of the United States: Harry S. Truman, 1947* (Washington, D.C., 1963), pp. 178–79. Note that the portions of Truman's message reproduced in the President's memoirs, *Year of Trial and Hope* (Garden City, 1956), p. 106, and in Acheson's *Present at the Creation*, p. 297, have been artfully pruned of the more provocative verbiage.

55. Margaret Truman, *Harry S. Truman* (New York, 1973), p. 343.

56. Elsey to Clark Clifford, 8 March 1947, Elsey MSS, Box 17 (Truman Library). Emphasis added. George Kennan likewise despaired over the blatant ideological tone of the message, *Memoirs*, 2 vols. (Boston, 1967–72), pp. 1, 314–15, 319–20. Cf. Joseph M. Jones, *The Fifteen Weeks* (New York, 1955), pp. 151–55.

57. See Krock, *New York Times*, 23 March 1947.

58. *New York Times*, 18 May 1947, p. 20. Also see Byrnes' speech to the House of Bishops of the Protestant Episcopal Church, reported in the *New York Times*, 6 November 1947 in which he stated that he

still adhered to the position that is was "possible for us to get along with the Soviets. . . . Certainly we must try to do so."

Byrnes' basic disagreement with Truman as to how to deal with Russia has been all but overlooked in studies of the Cold War. In this respect, Byrnes may have been his own worst enemy. For as the Cold War intensified under Truman's leadership, and as Byrnes himself moved to the right in his subsequent career, it became difficult for him and others to accept the fact that he had ever advocated a conciliatory stance toward the Soviet Union.

59. *Present at the Creation,* p. 295. The *Foreign Relations of the United States* omits reference to the cable traffic between the U.S. delegation in Moscow and Washington pertaining to Truman's speech. But, see Department of State Decimal File 1326, White to McDermott, 13 March 1947 (740.00119); also ibid., p. 1318, Acheson to Marshall, 11 March 1947 (740.00119).

60. Clay's departure from Moscow reflected a deep division in the U.S. delegation over how Germany should be treated. If worst came to worst, and territorial revisions were made in the West to favor France, Clay wished to be back in Germany so that he could resign from there in protest. Personal interview, 14 February 1970.

61. *Clay Papers, 1,* 340–41. (Emphasis added.) Brown was a close friend of Clay's and of Secretary Byrnes and president of radio station WORD in Spartanburg, S.C.

62. Compare Clay's letter to Marshall of 2 May 1947 which analyzes the economic problems facing Germany (and which makes no reference to Soviet behavior) with Marshall's response (24 June 1947) which stressed "the difficulties imposed by Soviet refusal to cooperate." Clay's reply of 28 June 1947 likewise omits reference to Soviet actions. The fact is that Clay considered the demands of the nations of western Europe, particularly France, as far more serious. *Clay Papers, 1,* 346–49, 377–81; *Foreign Relations of the United States 2* (1947):931.

63. TT 8362, 24 July 1947, *Clay Papers, 1,* 385–88.

64. Eisenhower to Clay [W-82808], 25 July 1947, Personal Files, General Lucius D. Clay, Modern Military Records, (U.S. National Archives). [Bracketed figures are cable numbers.]

65. Clay to Eisenhower [CC-1046], 28 July 1947. Reprinted in *Clay Papers, 1,* 389–90.

66. On 27 October 1947, Clay advised Washington that "the Western march of Communism has been stopped in central Germany." He sincerely believed that the ideals of American democracy had found roots in Germany and that they would survive provided the German population could be assured a reasonable standard of living. "We do not need to fear for democracy in Western Germany," he said. Clay to Royall, 27 October 1947 (CC 2103); *Clay Papers, 1,* 446–48.

Clay's commitment to teaching democracy caused him to resist Washington's efforts to outlaw the Communist Party in the U.S. zone. "I can think of no more undemocratic thing than to suppress the Communist Party . . . and I have no intention of doing so," he told a press conference on 28 October 1947. See *Clay Papers, 1*, 451, 456; also see Clay for Royall, 20 September 1947 (CC 1667), ibid., p. 431.

67. *Foreign Relations of the United States* 2 (1947):770–72. (The report of Marshall's action is exceedingly sketchy in this volume. We are informed however, that Truman backed Marshall to the hilt.) "Your firm and constructive [sic] actions in London have my complete support," he cabled Marshall on December 11. Ibid., p. 764.

68. See *Foreign Relations of the United States* 2 (1947):811–30.

69. See *New York Times*, 9 January 1948.

70. Stimson Diary, 31 March 1945 (Yale). Also see Jean Edward Smith, "Selection of a Proconsul for Germany: The Appointment of General Lucius D. Clay, 1945," *Military Affairs* 40 (1976):123–29.

71. Kennan, *Memoirs*, pp. 1, 401–03. Also see the extensive treatment in Bennet Kovrig, *The Myth of Liberation* (Baltimore, 1968), p. 82.

72. *Clay Papers, 2*, 568–69.

73. *Forrestal Diaries*, p. 387.

74. George Kennan noted its effect and cautiously indicates his disagreement with Clay's analysis. But, of course, Kennan believed Clay's message to be a genuine assessment of Soviet intent. *Memoirs*, p. 400.

75. On March 5, Clay sent a much more sober assessment to Henry Cabot Lodge. Similarly, on March 3, he advised the Department of the Army that he did not believe "there was an immediate danger of war with Russia." See *Clay Papers, 2*, 564–68.

76. The following week, when Under Secretary Draper requested a statement from Clay to be used in the appropriations hearings, Clay declined, reminding Draper that he had already sent a statement to Chamberlain for that purpose.

77. "Governor-General of Germany," loc. cit., fn. 7.

78. D. Robinson, "They Fight the Cold War under Cover," *Saturday Evening Post*, 20 November 1948.

79. Clay to Bradley (CC 7137) 20 December 1948, *Clay Papers, 2*, 961–62 (emphasis added). In his memoirs Clay is plainly embarrassed by the March 5 cable. "Having used carefully restrained language in which there was no indication of military action," he wrote with less than candor, "I did not consider it alarmist." *Decision in Germany*, pp. 354–55.

80. See, for example, the discussion of the impact of Clay's cable in Millis and Kennan, notes 71 and 72, supra.

81. Kennan, *Memoirs*, p. 401. Also see John Gimbel, *The American Occupation of Germany*, p. 204.

82. See, for example, Frank Howley's *Berlin Command* (New York,

1950), an emotional diatribe dedicated to his wife and four children who withstood "the daily insults, threats, and privations of Communist rats who walked like bears." Phillips Davidson's more elaborate analysis for the RAND Corporation, *The Berlin Blockade: A Study in Cold War Politics* (Princeton, 1958), is as Professor Gaddis Smith of Yale has suggested, "a veritable cold warrior's handbook." The present author's treatment of the blockade in *The Defence of Berlin* suffers from a similar failing.

83. TT-9667 (Clay to Royall), 25 June 1948, *Clay Papers*, 2, 699–704.
84. See *Clay Papers*, 2, 611, 639–42, et seq.
85. Clay to Draper (CC-4875), 25 June 1948; Clay to Bradley (CC 5118) 10 July 1948; TT-9766, 12 July 1948; TT-9768, 13 July 1948. *Clay Papers*, 2, 696–97, et seq.
86. "The Berlin Blockade through the Filter of History," loc. cit., p. 51.

5

Cold War Historians and the Occupation of Germany

John Gimbel
Humboldt State University

Historians of the Cold War have consistently documented their studies with illustrations from Soviet-American relations in postwar Germany. One historian, Ronald Steel, went so far as to state that the Cold War began with Russian-American disputes over Germany.[1] Herbert Feis claimed Germany was "the primary scene and cause of discord" between the two powers,[2] and Barton Bernstein saw Germany as the "key issue in the Cold War struggle."[3] William McNeill said that Germany's central position in Europe, her technical skills, her coal and industrial products, and her potential military power "all combined to make Germany the chief prize to be won in Europe, or, indeed, in the world."[4]

Cold War historians are often classified as traditionalists, revisionists, cold warriors, or adherents of the New Left. Each of the groups is, of course, subject to further subdivision, based on emphasis, self-imposed topical limitation, and objectives. The authors also differ in their research skills, the subtlety of their arguments, and the refinement of their exposition. Many have also been limited by source unavailability at the time they wrote.[5]

The traditionalists, or orthodox cold warriors, of whom Herbert Feis, John W. Spanier, and Arthur M. Schlesinger, Jr., are examples,[6] generally attribute the collapse of the wartime coalition and the origins of the

Cold War to Russian initiatives in the postwar world: the Russians had taken liberties in Poland and Eastern Europe. The Russians refused to withdraw from Iran and finally did so only under strong American pressure. They inspired revolutionary movements in Eastern Europe and Greece. They supported Communist parties in Italy, France, and in the Soviet occupation zone of Germany. In Germany they caused the failure of four-power control: they would not agree to establish central German administrations, treat Germany as an economic unit, or adopt common export-import policies for the four zones. Furthermore, they removed reparations unilaterally and pushed radical land reform, socialization, and one-party rule in their zone.

The traditionalists argue that Americans (and their allies) responded to the various Russian initiatives—first hesitatingly, then piecemeal, and finally with a containment program. The accounts follow a pattern. Franklin D. Roosevelt had hoped to cooperate with the Russians after the war. Some cold warriors think he made unreasonable concessions at Teheran and Yalta. Others defend him for doing what was historically necessary and morally proper but note that he had become disillusioned with the Russians at the time of his death in April 1945. Traditionalists agree that Harry S. Truman took a firm stand. He listened to hard-liners, such as W. Averell Harriman, James V. Forrestal, Henry L. Stimson, and William D. Leahy. Following their advice, he lectured Soviet Foreign Minister V. M. Molotov on Poland eleven days after taking office. He told Secretary of State James F. Byrnes in January 1946 that he was "through babying the Soviets." In March 1946, he accompanied Winston Churchill to Fulton, Missouri, where the latter gave the Iron Curtain speech. Following Truman's lead in Washington and George F. Kennan's analysis of the sources of Soviet conduct (beginning with the long telegram of February 22, 1946), Americans got tough in Germany. General Lucius D. Clay stopped reparations shipments from the American zone in May 1946, and Clay and Byrnes pushed for a revival of Western Germany in the summer and fall. On September 6, 1946, Byrnes made a policy speech in Stuttgart, Germany and set forth the outlines of a program for German recovery and rehabilitation. Byrnes' speech foreshadowed the policy of containment—a policy described and justified by Kennan in his famous Mr. X article in *Foreign Affairs* for July 1947 and a policy implemented by the Truman Doctrine, a new directive on Germany, and the Marshall Plan.

The Cold War revisionists, of whom William A. Williams, Gar Alperovitz, Gabriel Kolko, Lloyd C. Gardner, and Bruce Kuklick are examples,[7] see things differently. For the most part, they examine the same events that the traditionalists do, but they assign primary responsibility for the collapse of the wartime coalition to the United States rather than to the Soviet Union. They argue that Americans used economic warfare and the implied threat of their atomic monopoly to try to dictate a postwar settlement in Eastern Europe. Americans wanted a world economy characterized by the open door and multilateral trade. They wanted an economy that Americans could easily dominate by virtue of their advanced industrial plant, which had not suffered from wartime destruction. In the long run, the United States wanted to undo the Russian Revolution and bring Communism into eclipse.

Revisionist historians assign importance to Truman's personality, to his sense of righteousness, to his small-town, country-judge mentality, and to his lack of experience in foreign affairs. They judge him to have been at the mercy of his hard-line advisers (Harriman, Leahy, Stimson, Forrestal), many of whom had failed to get through to his more experienced and sophisticated predecessor. Revisionists focus on Truman's tongue-lashing of Molotov on April 23, 1945; on his abrupt cancellation of lend-lease shipments in May; on his decision to drop the atomic bomb; on American intentions regarding Eastern Europe; on the failure of the United States to advance a $6 billion postwar reconstruction credit to the Soviet Union; on Clay's and Byrnes' initiatives in Germany in the summer and fall of 1946; on the American opposition to Socialism in Germany; on the Truman Doctrine; and on the Marshall Plan.

Although their *analyses* differ sharply, traditionalist and revisionist Cold War historians generally agree in their *descriptions* of key events in the occupation of Germany. But, as I shall note later, many of these descriptions are inaccurate and distorted. The thesis of this paper is that Cold War historians have focused too sharply on Soviet-American confrontations in their interpretations and descriptions of the American occupation, and they have ignored or minimized the influence of the French, the British, the American Congress, and the American bureaucracy. Historians have used the Cold War not as a term to classify an historical condition or situation, but as an analytical tool and an organizational principle. The concept "Cold War" has become a ready-made standard for certain writers and researchers to arrange complex historical phenomena into a clear, manageable pattern. In short, historians have brought the "Cold War" to the data, and they have been blind to interpretations of events that do not fit a Cold War pattern. Thus, the key events of the German occupation have been divorced from their original context and placed into patterns that illustrate the evolution and nature of the Cold War. The result is that certain events have become *historic*, but they have ceased to be *historical*. I propose to illustrate this condition by looking at four events from the American occupation of Germany: General Clay's suspension of reparations deliveries from the American zone; Secretary of States Byrnes' invitation of July 11, 1946, which led to the formation of the British-American bizone; Byrnes' German policy speech of September 6, 1946 in Stuttgart, Germany; and Secretary of State George C. Marshall's speech at Harvard University on June 5, 1947, which inspired the Marshall Plan and brought forth a new Joint Chiefs of Staff directive on Germany in July 1947.

Clay's Reparations Suspension

On May 3, 1946, General Clay announced in the Allied Control Council in Berlin that he was stopping further reparations deliveries from the American zone in Germany.

Cold War historians have interpreted Clay's reparations suspension as a move against the Soviet Union.[8] They differ greatly in their discussion of causes and motives. Traditional cold warriors see the reparations halt as a response to Soviet unilateral reparations removals, to Soviet unwillingness to treat Germany as an economic unit, and to Soviet rejection of a German export-import program that would have helped to reduce American dollar outlays for the prevention of disease and unrest in Germany. Some cold warriors see Clay's action as a belated, yet welcome, rejection of the spirit of the Morgenthau Plan and of Roosevelt's vain hope of postwar cooperation with the Soviet Union.[9]

Revisionist historians interpret Clay's action as an attempt to deny Russia a legitimate share of Germany's reparations payments. It was a move to force the German economy into a multilateral trade world ripe for American economic exploitation and a symbol of America's determination to rebuild Germany as a bulwark against the Soviet Union.[10] Together with Truman's cancellation of lend-lease shipments to Russia and the decision not to provide Russia with a $6 billion postwar credit, the reparations suspension is seen by revisionists as an attempt to frustrate Russia's postwar economic recovery. In this view, the reparations stop was a victory for American anti-Soviet hard-liners, many of whom wanted to rebuild Germany as a bulwark against Russia.

But these conclusions are not supported by the documents and records of the event. Clay did not stop reparations to Russia alone, and he said so at least twice within a month—once in answer to a reporter's question in a press conference and a second time in a cable to the War Department.[11] Clay stopped reparations from going to all recipients, including France, Yugoslavia, Belgium, the Netherlands, Czechoslovakia, and a handful of other countries. It is pertinent to note that Clay's major problems in the Control Council at the time were with the French—not with the Russians. The French were blocking economic unity and vetoing the creation of central German administrations. Robert Murphy, the State Department's political adviser in Berlin, had reported—almost exactly a month before the reparations suspension—that it was the French who were sabotaging the Potsdam Agreement.[12] It should come as no surprise, therefore, that even *after* his reparations suspension, Clay reported to Washington that the Russians would probably cooperate in Berlin but that the French would not.[13]

If the reparations stop was against everybody and not particularly against the Russians, it needs to be reinterpreted. I suggest that it was a tactic to jolt the State Department in Washington. The evidence seems rather convincing. The French had been refusing to cooperate in the Control Council since September 1945. Immediately after the Potsdam Conference, France demanded decisions on the future of the Saar, the Ruhr, and the Rhineland (France wanted to annex the Saar and separate the Ruhr and Rhineland from Germany), and French representatives in Berlin blocked every action that France thought might prejudice the future of these three areas. Clay and the War Department had tried in vain since October 1945 to get the State Department to put pressure on France to implement the Potsdam Agreement. The State Department stalled, delayed, procrastinated, tried to shift blame on the Russians, and expressed polite concern to France, rather than apply the kind of political and economic sanctions Clay and the War Department asked for.[14] Finally, in May 1946, Clay interrupted the ongoing discussions on various economic issues in the Control Council to announce a halt in reparations deliveries. He said he had to know whether economic unity, one of the assumptions of the Control Council's reparations plan, would prevail. His purpose was to force a government-level discussion on Germany's future and France's vetoes of central German agencies.[15]

The State Department's immediate response to Clay's reparations suspension is evidence in support of this interpretation. Dean G. Acheson and John H. Hilldring tried to get Clay to resume reparations deliveries for 60 to 90 days. In the interim, they proposed "to put Soviet protestations of loyalty to Potsdam to [the] final test in order to gauge their willingness to live up to the substance as well as the letter of Potsdam and fix blame for [the] breach of Potsdam on [the] Soviets in case they fail to meet this test."[16] This is what John L. Gaddis referred to as smoking out the Russians.[17] The Acheson-Hilldring proposal, reflecting the State Department's tendency to want to protect France from the United States army, made passing reference to the technical legitimacy of France's vetoes, based on the fact that France had not been a partner to the Potsdam negotiations and Agreement. It suggested various concessions to France and expressed belief in French acceptance, significantly ignoring the fact that Georges Bidault's objections were already a matter of record. Interestingly, the proposal contained no precise information on Russia's failure to cooperate, but it was replete with speculations on Russian intentions.

Byrnes' Invitation to Zonal Union

On July 11, 1946, at the Council of Foreign Ministers meeting in Paris, Secretary of State Byrnes invited all other occupation powers in Germany to join their zones with the American zone to form an economic unit.

Cold War historians see Byrnes' invitation as a significant event in the history of the Cold War. John L. Gaddis, for example, wrote that "Byrnes . . . became convinced that the Russians would never allow implementation of the Potsdam Accords, and from this time on moved toward the concept of a divided Germany as the only alternative to a Russian-dominated Reich."[18]

Cold warriors see Byrnes' invitation as he described it in 1946 and 1947 as a hesitant move toward German rehabilitation and economic self-sufficiency and as a last resort.[19] They see it as a necessary consequence of the failure of the Control Council to develop German central economic administrations and to treat Germany as an economic unit. Since they also blame the Soviet Union for those failures, they are, in fact, arguing that Byrnes' invitation was prompted by the Russians.[20]

Revisionists see it otherwise. They regard Byrnes' invitation as a decision to rebuild Germany, even if it resulted in Germany's division. Some of them see it as an American attempt to gain effective control over the British zone in order to prevent socialization of the Ruhr industries. Some see it as an American attempt to coopt Britain and France. Americans wanted zonal union so they could coordinate British and French policies with American plans for German economic rehabilitation and the creation of a West German state under American guidance and tutelage. In an even larger sense, revisionists see Byrnes' invitation as indicative of the American thrust toward world economic hegemony via the open door and multilateral trade programs.[21]

But these conclusions are not supported by the documents of the event. The records show that Byrnes' invitation was tactical rather than strategic. It was hastily conceived and reflective of past failures rather than of future plans, and it was defensive toward Britain, rather than offensive toward the Soviet Union. Byrnes issued the invitation as an immediate response to an announcement by British Foreign Secretary Ernest Bevin that, in the absence of four-power agreement on a British import-export plan for *all* of Germany, Britain would develop a self-sufficient economic program in its own zone.[22] Byrnes' invitation begins with these words: "I hope we can avoid the situation outlined by Mr. Bevin. . . ."[23]

The history of Byrnes' invitation has been skewed by Byrnes' own accounts of it. He said he listened to Molotov's German policy speech on July 10th, then he and his advisers huddled with Senators Arthur Vandenberg and Tom Connally that night. Together they decided to issue the invitation, which had been planned as a last resort. The official historian of Byrnes' secretaryship (George Curry) said that Byrnes issued the invitation the next morning.[24] As a matter of fact, however, the invitation was not issued in the morning. It came at the very end of a full day of deliberations, during which Byrnes continued to press for appointment of special deputies to *study* the German questions for the *next* meeting of the Council of Foreign Ministers. In the end, he agreed to a compromise to delay their appointment until the fall. Byrnes' invitation came after all that, at the end of the day, and as a counterproposal to the statement by Bevin that he would have to move independently in the British zone to cut dollar costs to the British. That is why Byrnes said: "I hope that we can avoid the situation outlined by Mr. Bevin. . . ."[25]

Other evidence is also pertinent. The preparatory materials Byrnes took with him to Paris in the summer of 1946 apparently contained no working papers or policy proposals devoted to a possible invitation for zonal union such as he issued. This suggests that the matter of a West German solution was not seriously considered as *policy* at the time. Of course, there is always the possibility that James P. Warburg was right when he said that Byrnes carried "the State Department around the world in his brief case," and that some of these things never got back into the archives.[26] In any case, only after Byrnes issued the invitation orally in Paris did the State Department in Washington quickly draft the formal invitation and related policy guidance documents for use by the American military governor in the Control Council in Berlin.[27] It would seem, therefore, that Byrnes "shot from the hip" in response to Bevin, and policy followed improvised action. There is no evidence that Byrnes went to Paris with preconceived plans for rebuilding Germany, for dividing Germany, or for "dishing" the Russians.

Byrnes' Stuttgart Speech

Secretary of State Byrnes left the Paris Peace Conference in the fall of 1946 and went to Germany, where he delivered a major policy speech in Stuttgart on September 6, 1946, before the minister-presidents of the U.S. zone.

Cold War historians agree that Byrnes' speech was a landmark of American policy and that it signaled the permanent division of Germany. They agree that Byrnes formally renounced the more stringent provisions of JCS 1067 and the Morgenthau Plan and that he called into question certain provisions of the Potsdam Agreement. They further agree that Byrnes made overtures to the Germans about reduced occupation controls and a future German government. John L. Gaddis echoed all of these views when he said: "Byrnes' Stuttgart speech represented an important reversal of the American position on Germany."[28]

Cold warriors and revisionists differ in their analyses of Byrnes' motives, in the same way that they differ on Clay's reparations suspension and Byrnes' invitation to zonal union. Traditionalists see the speech as an American response to Russian behavior in Berlin and to Molotov's German policy speech of July 10, 1946 in Paris.[29] Revisionists see it as an American initiative, in keeping with the larger postwar foreign policy of the Truman Administration. For the revisionists, the speech is an official announcement that the United States would rebuild Germany as a base for maintaining American influence in Europe. It is in keeping with the American desire to rebuild a German free enterprise economy, open to American conceptions of mutilateralism, and fertile for American investments and trade. In the words of Lloyd C. Gardner, it was Byrnes' speech that "put the U.S. on the political and ideological offensive in Germany." He said "Byrnes wanted to deliver a speech that would embarrass the Russians . . . finesse the French . . . [and] smite the Socialist bogeyman directly."[30]

The documents and records of the event permit a different conclusion. Byrnes did want to match Molotov's July 10th policy statement, which was getting much attention in Germany. Molotov had declared the Ruhr to be German, and Byrnes matched him by making clear that the United States would not agree to France's demands for separation of the Ruhr and the Rhineland. Byrnes went on to outline and comment on United States policy, but there was little that was new. This is evident from the fact that the speech follows almost exactly a policy *summary* Clay had prepared for release in Berlin in July 1946.[31] The State Department had vetoed Clay's proposal to publish the summary at the time. Thereupon Clay visited Byrnes in Paris and urged him to make a policy statement so

American officials in Germany could use it as leverage to promote a program to achieve economic unity by encouraging meetings and conferences of the German minister-presidents and other officials of the four zones. In short, Byrnes intended the speech for German and French ears more than he did for Russian ears. Only later, particularly after his showdown with Henry A. Wallace over the latter's Madison Square Garden speech of September 12, 1946, did Byrnes regard his Stuttgart speech as though it had been addressed to the Soviet Union. The evidence for these conclusions is to be found within the text of the speech, in the conditions and incidents that led to its delivery, and in the way it was received in France. A discussion of these things is beyond the scope of this paper, but it is contained in an article that I published not long ago, both in the United States and in Germany.[32]

Marshall's Harvard Speech of June 5, 1947

As they have misinterpreted other episodes and events described in this paper, historians in search of the Cold War in Germany have misinterpreted the context out of which the Marshall Plan emerged. When Secretary of State George C. Marshall spoke at the Harvard commencement on June 5, 1947, he had no plan for European recovery, for containment of Communism, for creating a multilateral trade world, for promoting the open-door policy in Europe, or for forestalling a postwar recession in the United States. He had a practical problem that he thought would have to be resolved before someone else with "all kinds of bright and unworkable ideas" tried to do so.[33]

Marshall's practical problem was in Germany, where France's vetoes in the Allied Control Council had effectively prevented the creation of central German economic administrations since 1945. Faced with the impasse caused by France's vetoes and appalled at the high cost of the occupation in appropriated dollars, the army and Clay had maneuvered for two years to try to bring France around. But the State Department, influenced especially by H. Freeman Matthews, Benjamin V. Cohen, and Dean G. Acheson, had refused either to apply sanctions against France or to admit publicly that France was indeed the major problem in Germany. Instead, State Department functionaries expressed suspicions about Russian intentions and long-range objectives in Germany, and they did so despite Clay's and Murphy's evidence and arguments that the Russians were cooperating in Berlin to fulfill the terms of the Potsdam Agreement. Eventually, after Clay forced the issue by suspending reparations shipments from the American zone, the State Department devised a test of Russian intentions and then proceeded to accuse the Russians of violating the Potsdam Agreement.[34]

Meanwhile, the Russians went their own way in their zone. The British, who needed even more desperately than the army to reduce occupation costs in Germany, threatened several times to adopt unilateral policies in their own zone. As noted above, Bevin outlined a British plan in July 1946, to promote a self-sufficient economy in the British zone, which included the Ruhr. Searching for an alternative, Byrnes invited all the occupation powers to join their zones with the American zone in economic unity. Britain eventually accepted Byrnes' invitation, but France and Russia did not. Britain and the army expected zonal union to result in substantial reductions in the financial burdens of the occupation, and the two military governors developed a three-year plan to make the bizone self-supporting by 1949. But the State Department, which made policy for the United States in Germany, would not agree to economic policies in bizonal Germany that impinged on its own plans for rehabilitating liberated Europe first. Neither would the State Department approve bizonal policies and practices that threatened France's postwar recovery plans and political stability, or that left France's expectations for German coal exports unfulfilled. Specifically, the State Department objected to a bizonal policy that would have required Germany's customers to pay cash for such things as coal, timber, and transit services, all of which had been leaving Germany since 1945 as "hidden reparations."

Early in 1947 the army and the British got an ally. The Republican leaders of the newly elected Eightieth Congress were determined to cut costs and to wrest power from the executive branch, i.e., from the Democratic Administration. Some were prepared to investigate the reasons for the "failure" in Germany; some were prepared to review the State Department's wartime and postwar stewardship of American foreign policy; and many were spoiling for a political showdown with the party of the New Deal.

Faced with Congress' inclination to intervene in the German occupation, with the army's continued restlessness, with the failure of the foreign ministers to make progress on a German peace settlement at the Moscow Conference, and with a British decision of January 1947 to increase German steel production, Marshall moved to solve the economic problems of the bizone by moderating State Department opposition to British and U.S. army objectives. During the Council of Foreign Ministers meeting in Moscow, he and Bevin compromised hitherto irreconcilable positions by agreeing privately to reorganize the bizone administratively, to raise the bizonal level of industry, and to make the two zones self-sustaining

95

by 1949.[35] Marshall was prompted to give way to this extent by his knowledge of Clay's problems, by Bevin's determination to reduce British dollar costs in Germany, and by information that Herbert Hoover's recent recommendations for a new economic policy in Germany strongly appealed to members of Congress, and to such key colleagues in the cabinet as Secretary of Commerce W. Averell Harriman, Secretary of Navy James V. Forrestal, Secretary of Agriculture Clinton P. Anderson, Secretary of War Robert P. Patterson, and Budget Director James E. Webb.[36] Patterson had, in fact, already declared that the army would use Hoover's recommendations as the basis for the War Department's budget requests in Congress.[37]

Yet, Marshall's misgivings about the new course remained sufficiently strong to prevent an immediate overt reversal of United States policy. Sensing that his and Bevin's decision to reorganize the bizone, to raise the German level of industry, and to reduce Germany's coal and timber exports would cause political repercussions at home and abroad, Marshall prevailed upon Bevin to delay announcement of their agreement for about six weeks. Upon further reflection, and after consultations with Clay, John Foster Dulles, and other State Department advisers, Marshall concluded that the German decisions he and Bevin had made in Moscow were politically dangerous and unwise. While they might solve the German economic problem, they would do so at political costs that his own department thought were too high. The Moscow-German decisions threatened to cause political disaster in France. They would certainly bring heavy criticism from France, Russia, anti-German hard-liners in the United States (such as Henry Morgenthau and the Society for the Prevention of World War III), liberal press in the United States (such as *PM* and the *New Republic*), and liberals, leftists, Communists, and anti-Germans everywhere. Unwilling to face charges that the United States planned to restore its recently defeated enemy ahead of its friends and allies, Marshall decided that his commitment to Bevin would have to be modified, and that the army's, Hoover's and the Congress' plans for German recovery would have to be headed off.

True to his training and experience—and perhaps to his instincts as well—Marshall called for the equivalent of military staff-studies on his problem. Immediately upon his return from the Moscow Conference, he instructed George F. Kennan to activate the Policy Planning Staff in the State Department and to prepare the studies that eventually became the basis for the Marshall Plan. Kennan and the Policy Planning Staff resolved Marshall's dilemma by recommending first, a short-term program—"coal for Europe"—that would do in Germany essentially what he and Bevin had already decided to do in Moscow, and second, a long-term program of European economic recovery to be developed by the Europeans themselves but with friendly aid from the United States.[38] According to the Policy Planning Staff, the former—which has been completely ignored by historians—would be merged with the latter as soon as possible. This would diffuse domestic criticism of Germany's recovery and help insure against the economic and political disaster a "Germany first" program threatened to call forth, particularly in France, but not exclusively there. The Policy Planning Staff paper of May 23, 1947—which contributed measurably to Marshall's Harvard speech—was, in fact, a plan to implement the German decisions Marshall and Bevin had already made. These decisions raised the specter of a restored Germany equipped with the manpower, resources, and technical facilities Germans had used with such profound effect in the past.

As Marshall said over and over, and as I have demonstrated in a book just published, there was no "Marshall Plan" on June 5, 1947, when Marshall spoke at Harvard. There was no plan for European recovery, for containment of Communism, for creating a multilateral trade world, for promoting the open-door policy in Europe, or for forestalling a postwar recession in the United States. Late in June 1947, when Under Secretary of State William L. Clayton went to Europe for consultations on the Harvard speech, he had specific instructions about a German-based "coal for Europe" program and about how to get the British to back off their plans to socialize coal production in the Ruhr, but he had only vague and general conceptions of what was to become the European recovery program.[39] As a matter of fact, his and Kennan's fundamental disagreements on the Policy Planning Staff recommendations of May 23, 1947 had not even been reconciled. As late as August 1947, State Department functionaries discussed these differences and talked about the need "to firm up the overall departmental position."[40] In the end, the Marshall Plan just grew. It evolved out of the give and take among Congress, the Truman Administration, and the Europeans themselves.

The only plans that existed in the summer and fall of 1947 were those Marshall and Bevin had made during the Moscow Conference: to reorganize the bizonal administration, to raise the level of industry, and to make the bizone self-sustaining. Those plans raised a spectrum of actual and potential domestic and foreign problems that would have to be resolved, diffused, and—if necessary—kept from the arena of public discussion and debate, at least for a time. How these things were done— how the Marshall Plan evolved from the Moscow decisions on Germany— is beyond the scope of this paper. But it should be clear from what has been given here, that the remarks made by Marshall at Harvard on June 5, 1947 are not clarified contextually by considering them to be primarily an aspect of the Cold War with the Soviet Union. Cold War historians are as wrong about the origins of the Marshall Plan as they are about the other events identified in this paper.

I might note, in closing, that once Molotov left the Paris three-power talks (with Bevin and Bidault) on the implementation of Marshall's Harvard speech, the planning for a European recovery program took on a rather distinct Cold War character. Not before, however, and it is wrong for historians to assign purposes and motives to Marshall by reading what members of Congress and newspapermen had to say on European recovery after the Russians had eliminated themselves from the program.

NOTES

1. Ronald Steel, *Pax Americana* (New York, 1967), p. 100.
2. Herbert Feis, *From Trust to Terror: The Onset of the Cold War, 1945–1950* (New York, 1970), p. 62.
3. Barton J. Bernstein, "American Foreign Policy and the Origins of the Cold War," in Bernstein, ed., *Politics and Policies of the Truman Administration* (Chicago, 1970), p. 51.
4. William H. McNeill, *America, Britain, and Russia: Their Cooperation and Conflict, 1941–1946* (London, 1953), p. 724. Similar examples include Louis J. Halle, *The Cold War as History* (New York, 1967), p. 32, and Hans J. Morgenthau, "Peace in Our Time?" *Commentary* 37 (1964):66.
5. For representative discussions of differences and for attempts to classify writers into "schools," see Charles S. Maier, "Revisionism and the Interpretation of Cold War Origins," *Perspectives in American History* 4 (1970):313–47; Christopher Lasch, "The Cold War, Revisited and Revisioned," *New York Times Magazine*, 14 January 1968, pp. 26–27++; Norman A. Graebner, "Cold War Origins and the Continuing Debate: A Review of Recent Literature," *The Journal of Conflict Resolution* 13 (1969):123–32; Paul Seabury, "Cold War Origins, I," *The Journal of Contemporary History* 3 (1968):168–82; Brian Thomas, "Cold War Origins, II," ibid., 183–98; Geoffrey Williams and Joseph Frankel, "A Political Scientists's Look at the Cold War as History," *Political Studies* 16 (1968):285–92; William W. MacDonald, "The Revisionist Cold War Historians," *The Midwest Quarterly* 9 (1969):37–49; Robert James Maddox, "Cold War Revisionism: Abusing History," *Freedom at Issue*, No. 15 (September–October 1972):3–6; D. F. Fleming, "When Did the Cold War Begin?" *The Nation*, 15 April 1968, pp. 508–10; Hans J. Morgenthau, "Arguing

About the Cold War: A Balance Sheet," *Encounter* 28 (May 1967): 37–41; and William A. Williams, "The Cold-War Revisionists," *The Nation*, 13 November 1967, pp. 492–95.

6. Feis, *From Trust to Terror*; John W. Spanier, *American Foreign Policy Since World War II*, Second Revised Edition (New York, 1965); Arthur M. Schlesinger, Jr., "Origins of the Cold War," *Foreign Affairs* 46 (1967):22–52.

7. William A. Williams, *The Tragedy of American Diplomacy*, Revised and Enlarged Edition (New York, 1962); Gabriel Kolko, *The Politics of War: The World and United States Foreign Policy, 1943–1945* (New York, 1968); Joyce and Gabriel Kolko, *The Limits of Power: The World and United States Foreign Policy, 1945–1954* (New York, 1972); Gar Alperovitz, *Atomic Diplomacy: Hiroshima and Potsdam* (New York, 1965); Lloyd C. Gardner, *Architects of Illusion: Men and Ideas in American Foreign Policy, 1941–1949* (Chicago, 1970); Bruce Kuklick, *American Policy and the Division of Germany: The Clash with Russia over Reparations* (Ithaca, 1972).

8. See, for examples, Frederick H. Gareau, "Morgenthau's Plan for Industrial Disarmament in Germany," *The Western Political Quarterly* 14 (1961):526; Robert Cecil, "Potsdam and its Legends," *International Affairs* 46 (1970):459; McNeill, *America, Britain, and Russia*, pp. 725–26; Robert Slusser, ed., *Soviet Economic Policy in Postwar Germany* (New York, 1953), pp. xvii–xviii; W. W. Rostow, *The United States in the World Arena* (New York, 1960), pp. 190–91; Evan Luard, ed., *The Cold War* (New York, 1964), p. 21; Desmond Donnelly, *Struggle for the World* (London, 1965), p. 221; Rolf Badstübner and Siegfried Thomas, *Die Spaltung Deutschlands, 1945–1949* (Berlin, 1966), p. 146; Michael Balfour, *West Germany* (London, 1968), p. 154; Thomas G. Paterson, "The Economic Cold War: American Business and Economic Policy, 1945–1950," (unpublished Ph.D. diss., University of California, Berkeley, 1968), pp. 427–28; and Frank Spencer, "The United States and Germany in the Aftermath of War," *International Affairs* 44 (1968):58.

9. See, for examples, William A. Brown and Redvers Opie, *American Foreign Assistance* (Washington, 1953), p. 122; George Curry, "James F. Byrnes," in Robert H. Ferrell, ed., *The American Secretaries of State and Their Diplomacy*, (New York, 1965), pp. 14, 235; and George F. Kennan, *Memoirs, 1925–1950* (Boston, 1967), pp. 259–60.

10. See, for examples, Bruce Kuklick, *American Policy and the Division of Germany*, esp. pp. 214–17; Lloyd C. Gardner, "America and the German 'Problem,' 1945–1949," in Bernstein, ed., *Politics and Policies of the Truman Administration*, pp. 113–46, esp. pp. 132–36; Joyce and Gabriel Kolko, *The Limits of Power*, esp. pp. 138–41; and Richard M. Freeland, *The Truman Doctrine and the Origins of McCarthyism* (New York, 1972), p. 54.

11. Office of Military Government for Germany (U.S.) [hereafter OMGUS], Public Relations Office, Transcript of Clay Press Conference, 27 May 1946, National Archives [hereafter NA], OMGUS Papers, 1-1/4; OMGUS, from Clay, to War Department, 5 June 1946, NA, RG 165, Box 351, file WDSCA 387.6, Sec. II. The press conference transcript quotes Clay as saying the stoppage applied "to everybody," and the cable reads that the "stoppage of dismantling [was] not directed at any one nation."
12. Murphy to SecState, 4 April 1946, in Department of State, *Foreign Relations of the United States 1946* (Washington, 1969) 5, 536–37. [Hereafter cited as FRUS.]
13. Lucius D. Clay, *Decision in Germany* (Garden City, 1950), pp. 73–78; OMGUS to War Department, 26 May 1946, NA, OMGUS Papers, 177-3/3.
14. For a full discussion see John Gimbel, "On the Implementation of the Potsdam Agreement: An Essay on U.S. Postwar German Policy," *Political Science Quarterly* 87 (1972):242–69.
15. OMGUS to War Department, 3 May 1946, NA, OMGUS Papers, 427-2/3; Murphy to SecState, 6 May 1946, *FRUS*, 1946, V, 547–48; OMGUS to War Department, 5 June 1946, NA, RG 165, Box 351, file WDSCA 387.6, Sec. II. See also John H. Backer, *Priming the German Economy: American Occupational Policies, 1945–1948* (Durham, N.C., 1971), pp. 110–11.
16. Acheson and Hilldring to SecState, 9 May 1946, *FRUS*, 1946, V, 549–56, esp. 549.
17. John L. Gaddis, *The United States and the Origins of the Cold War, 1941–1947* (New York, 1972), p. 328.
18. Ibid., p. 330. See also Feis, *From Trust to Terror*, pp. 156–59; Dean G. Acheson, *Present at the Creation: My Years in the State Department* (New York, 1969), p. 260; David L. Glickman, *The Big 4 in Germany* (Washington, D.C., 1947), p. 17; Stefan Doernberg, *Die Geburt eines neuen Deutschland, 1945–1949* (Berlin, 1959), p. 109; and Basil Davidson, *Germany What Now? Potsdam—Partition, 1945–1949* (London, 1950), p. 59.
19. See, for examples, James F. Byrnes, Report on Paris CFM Meeting, 15 June–12 July 1946, in Department of State, *Making the Peace Treaties, 1941–1947* (Washington, 1947), appendix 7, esp. p. 109; James F. Byrnes, *Speaking Frankly* (New York, 1947), pp. 195–96; Feis, *From Trust to Terror*, pp. 134–35; and Curry, "James F. Byrnes," p. 235.
20. See, for examples, Backer, *Priming the German Economy*, pp. 129–31; Donald Watt, "Germany," in Evan Luard, ed., *The Cold War* (New York, 1964), p. 96; Philip Windsor, "The Occupation of Germany," *History Today* 13 (1963):79; Oron J. Hale, "The American Experiment in Germany," *The South Atlantic Quarterly* 54 (1955):300–01;

W. H. Chamberlin, "The Cold War: A Balance Sheet," *The Russian Review* 9 (1950):82; Ferenc A. Vali, *The Quest for a United Germany* (Baltimore, 1967), p. 16; and Walter B. Smith, *My Three Years in Moscow* (Philadelphia, 1950), p. 222.

21. See, for examples, Kuklick, *American Policy and the Division of Germany*, p. 220; Joyce and Gabriel Kolko, *The Limits of Power*, pp. 142–45; Freeland, *The Truman Doctrine and the Origins of McCarthyism*, p. 54; and Gardner, "America and the German 'Problem,' 1945–1949," p. 133, for the statement that Clay and Byrnes needed leverage against Britain and France.

22. *FRUS, 1946, II*, 896–98, 900.

23. *FRUS, 1946, II*, 897–98. See also Department of State, *United States Economic Policy Toward Germany* (Washington, D.C., 1946), pp. 148–49, for the press release of Byrnes' statement of 11 July 1946.

24. Curry, "James F. Byrnes," p. 235. See also Feis, *From Trust to Terror*, p. 135.

25. *FRUS, 1946, II*, 881–98, esp. 897–98 for quoted sentence.

26. James P. Warburg, *Germany, Key to France* (Cambridge, 1953), p. 39.

27. War Department to OMGUS, 18 July 1946, NA, RG 165, file WDSCA 014 Germany, Sec. IX. (Reprinted, in part, in *FRUS, 1946, V*, 578–79).

28. Gaddis, *The United States and the Origins of the Cold War*, p. 331. See also Wolfgang Friedman, *The Allied Military Government of Germany* (London, 1947), p. 188; Michael Balfour and John Mair, *Four-Power Control in Germany and Austria, 1945–1946* (London, 1956), pp. 141–42; Backer, *Priming the German Economy*, pp. 126–27; Feis, *From Trust to Terror*, p. 159; Frank Spencer, "The United States and Germany in the Aftermath of War," *International Affairs* 44 (1968):60–61; Gardner, "America and the German 'Problem,' 1945–1949," p. 134; Acheson, *Present at the Creation*, p. 260; Gareau, "Morgenthau's Plan for Industrial Disarmament in Germany," p. 526; Delbert Clark, *Again the Goose Step* (Indianapolis, 1949), p. 57; and Vali, *The Quest for a United Germany*, p. 17.

29. See especially, Curry, "James F. Byrnes," 248–49 and Feis, *From Trust to Terror*, p. 156.

30. Gardner, "America and the German 'Problem,' 1945–1949," p. 134. See also Ellis M. Zacharias, *Behind Closed Doors: The Secret History of the Cold War* (New York, 1950), p. 73; Bernstein, "American Foreign Policy and the Origins of the Cold War," p. 50; and Joyce and Gabriel Kolko, *The Limits of Power*, esp. p. 169.

31. Clay to Echols, War Department, 19 July 1946, NA, OMGUS Papers, 177-1/3. See Gimbel, J., *The American Occupation of Germany: Politics and the Military, 1945–1949* (Stanford, 1968), pp. 76–78, for a summary.

32. Gimbel, J., "On the Implementation of the Potsdam Agreement," pp. 242–69, which also recapitulates the salient points of the Wallace speech.
33. Joseph M. Jones, *The Fifteen Weeks* (21 February–5 June 1947) (New York, 1955), pp. 223–24. The words are Kennan's to Jones, in a summary of Marshall's instructions on the work of the Policy Planning Staff.
34. Acheson and Hilldring to SecState, 9 May 1946, *FRUS*, 1946, V, 549–55.
35. Marshall to Acheson, 19 April 1947, *FRUS*, 1947, *II*, 357–58.
36. Acheson to Marshall, 20 March 1947, *FRUS*, 1947, *II*, 394–95.
37. Teleconference, Washington-Berlin (Noce, CAD, and Clay and Draper, OMGUS), 5 March 1947, NA, RG 107, file ASW 430, Book 2.
38. Kennan to Acheson, 23 May 1947, *FRUS*, 1947, *III*, 223–30.
39. Memorandum of Clayton-Bevin Conversation, 24 June 1947, *FRUS*, 1947, *III*, 268–73.
40. Minutes of Meeting on Marshall "Plan," 22 August 1947, *FRUS*, 1947, *III*, 369–72.

6

Principal Issues in the U.S. Occupation of Austria, 1945–1948

Milton Colvin
Washington and Lee University

By 1941 neither the Western Allies nor the Soviets were exactly sure what should be the policy toward Austria after the defeat of Hitler. As early as 1941, Stalin had told Anthony Eden on his first visit to Moscow that Russia wanted an independent and sovereign Austria as part of any postwar planning, but beyond that he was vague. All interest focused on Germany. On the American side of the ocean there was drift. It is alleged that President Roosevelt in a private chat with Archbishop Francis J. Spellman of New York indicated a willingness to let a liberated Austria fall into the Soviet sphere of influence even if this meant a Communist government in Vienna, arguing that there was little that America or England could do to prevent it.[1]

Part of the reason, at least, for both these attitudes was the absence of any Austrian exile government. Chancellor Schuschnigg and his cabinet remained in Austria after the Anschluss as German prisoners. Much of what might have been the Austrian Socialist opposition was divided and in exile. Archduke Otto von Habsburg was in America and without any meaningful following. No one tried or could speak for Austria. Some sort of reemergence of an independent Austria seemed to make sense as a check on future German power, but this was more of an afterthought than a policy commitment.

In the spring of 1943 this began to change. In April 1943 a memorandum was prepared in the British Foreign Office entitled "The Future of Austria." It was written by Geoffrey Harrison and approved by Anthony Eden.[2] The memorandum outlined possible positions on the Austrian question. It was discussed in June 1943 by the War Cabinet, chaired by Winston Churchill. It was hoped that a statement could be formulated that would encourage Austrian resistance against the Nazis. The British idea of an independent Austria as part of a Danubian Confederation proved unacceptable to the Soviet Union, who wanted no part of any renewed *cordon sanitaire* diplomacy and said as much. The upshot was another British draft in which the future relationship of an independent Austria with her eastern neighbors was somewhat muted. This was sent to Washington and further modified there.

Austria, as such, was not on the agenda of the Moscow Conference which began on October 19, 1943. It came into play only as part of the German problem. At the insistence of the Russians, all references to the future relationship between Austria and her Danubian neighbors were dropped. Also, at Russian insistence, the Austrians were reminded that they had fought on Hitler's side and that Austria had a responsibility for this action "which she cannot escape."[3]

The full text of the Moscow Declaration was made public on November 1, 1943 and some two weeks later, the Free French Committee of General DeGaulle added its approval. In the Declaration, the Allies pledged themselves to work for the creation of a free and independent Austria, and the Austrians themselves were urged to take their own steps to bring about the defeat of Germany and warned that such action or lack of action would be taken into account in the final reckoning.

In a sense, the United States now had a commitment to Austria, but there still seemed to be little high-level interest in postwar planning. Indeed, President Roosevelt was not even sure whether the United States should keep forces in Austria beyond the few necessary to show the flag in Vienna.[4] True, the newly created European Advisory Commission (EAC) was empowered to work out general occupation policies to be implemented upon the collapse of the Third Reich, but the Commission seemed to be in no hurry to do much about Austria.

In a separate action in the spring of 1944, planning for the military government of Austria was undertaken by the Western Allies under an informal agreement between Supreme Headquarters, Allied Expeditionary Forces in England, and the Supreme Allied Commander in the Mediterranean in Italy. For the United States this meant there was a planning group under the War Department and another planning group working through the EAC. The division of authority and channels made for difficulties.

Serious discussion concerning zones and occupational control began in EAC meetings in late summer and early fall of 1944. At first, it looked like American representation would be limited to a token force in Vienna, and the rest of Austria would be divided between the British and the Soviets. However, in November of 1944 the Russians presented a plan which called for major American participation in the division of Austria. Professor Gerald Stourzh in his excellent short study of the development of the Austrian State Treaty suggests that the Soviets wanted the Americans in Austria to balance out British influence which they feared might check their own.[5] If so, it was a gross misjudgment on Moscow's part of postwar power relationships.

Two weeks before Christmas of 1944, President Roosevelt gave the green light to an American occupation zone in Austria to adjoin the American zone in Germany. In January 1945 the French indicated a desire for a zone in Austria as well as one in Germany and after much wrangling, particularly over division of sectors in Vienna, general agreement was reached, and Austria was divided into four zones. The Russians took the eastern part, including the area around Vienna, the British were in the south, the Americans and the French in the west. The date was July 9, 1945, two months after the end of the war and three months after the Russian capture of the capital. By then, events had already been set into motion which were to confront the Western Allies with some hard choices. Things had happened to Austrians which were to shift popular sympathy irrevocably to the West.

While the British, the Americans, and the French had been debating among themselves and with the Soviets about future zones and sectors in a not-yet-conqured Austria, the Red Army under Marshal Tolbukhin swept across the Hungarian plains and entered Austria on March 31, 1945. The Americans had crossed the Rhine but not yet bridged the Po. A week later, on April 7, the Russians were at the gates of Vienna, and the next day, Radio Moscow announced to the Austrians that the Soviets were coming to Austria as "liberators" and that the Soviet Union had no intention of appropriating any part of the Austrian territory or "changing the social order in any way."[6] It also urged resistance groups to sabotage German defensive positions in and around the city and to organize and help the Soviets drive the Nazis out of Austria.

Even this late in the game, however, no organized resistance movement existed in Vienna. Small groups did work effectively, but they were hardly a decisive force. Unlike 1918, when worker and soldier committees took power into their own hands, in April 1945 the majority of Viennese chose to hide in the cellars of their homes and wait out the battle for the control of the city. The end of the Third Reich in Austria was not due to internal collapse nor revolution in the streets but solely to the sledgehammer blows of the powerful Red Army. By the middle of April, the city of Vienna had been cleared of German forces and what was left of the German army in eastern Austria was retreating in considerable disorder toward the west.

In retrospect, it seems fairly certain that it was in the days and nights during the siege of Vienna that the Soviets threw away whatever chances they might have had of being greeted as "liberators." Russian troops raped and plundered as if they were true believers in the old battle slogan: "The bride to the victors." The Austrians were terror stricken. It was as if the Golden Horde had come among them. All the worst stories about the Russian soldiers were confirmed. Whether the Soviet High Command could not or would not control its troops is not really known. The same brutal and inexcusable behavior had marked the advance of the Red Army into Germany and, to a comparable extent, into Yugoslavia and Czechoslovakia. As far as the Austrians were concerned, this confirmed the Russians as barbarians and destroyed forever any real rapport between victor and vanquished. Even the Austrian Communists flown in from Moscow, well prepared and ably led, could never overcome this mass aversion. The Soviets erected a huge statue of the Red Army soldier which still dominates the Schwarzenbergplatz in downtown Vienna. Today, more than thirty years later, it is known to the Viennese as "the unknown rapist."

Besides driving the Germans from eastern Austria, the Soviets were successful in putting together a provisional government while "on the march." This provisional government was ultimately to get recognition from the Western Allies and to become the symbol of Austrian sovereignty during the period under review. It was a remarkable achievement, made even more remarkable by the fact that many of the men who were a part of it would soon be overtly and covertly doing their best to work against Soviet policy in Austria. The Soviets had, unknowingly, put together a Trojan horse, but an intelligent and patient Trojan horse, one well suited to the Austrian temperament.

As the Russians entered eastern Austria, they discovered in the small town of Gloggnitz Karl Renner, who in 1919 had been the Chancellor of the first Austrian Republic. He was a Socialist of non-Marxist persuasion, well respected throughout the country. To the Soviets he must have seemed an ideal figurehead. They latched onto him and sent him to Vienna and entrusted him with the job of forming a government. This he did, putting together a 13-man cabinet made up of Socialists, Communists, Conservatives of the People's Party, and two others without party identification. The Communists were given the portfolios of Interior (police) and Education. It was the standard Soviet formula for setting up a non-Communist government which could, with time and patience, be subverted by Communist intrigue. On April 27, 1945, Dr. Renner's provisional government declared the establishment of a "democratic Austrian Republic" based on the Austrian constitution of 1920.[7]

Three days later, on April 30, 1945, Churchill sent a message to President Truman expressing concern "about the way things are going in Austria."[8] He feared that the Soviets "were exploiting their arrival first into Austria in order to organize the country before the Western Allies arrive,"[9] and he urged President Truman to take a strong stand on the grounds that to do less would make it difficult to exercise any influence during the liberation. The same day both governments sent protest messages to the Soviets in regard to Soviet action in unilaterally establishing a provisional government of Austria.

By April 1945 it no longer appeared to the United States that entry into Austria would come from the Italian front. Instead, it was more realistic to expect the American drive across western Germany to sweep into Austria. This was fueled by a strong desire on the part of General Eisenhower to deny to the Germans any sort of last-ditch stand in the Berchtesgaden area of Bavaria which adjoined the western borders of Austria. With this in mind, a hasty transfer of responsibility for United States occupation in Austria was effected by which command control was taken from the Mediterranean Command and given to the European Theatre of Operations (London).

In early May it was unofficially given back, when the Headquarters of the 15th Army Group was selected to be Headquarters of United States forces in Austria. General Mark Clark was designated to be High Commissioner (on the Allied Council). His mandate was:

> . . . to be Commander in Chief of United States Forces of Occupation in Austria and to be responsible for political matters pertaining to Austria and for the administration of Military Government in Zone.[10]

By this time, of course, United States forces were in Austria, the war was over, and contact had been made by British and American troops with their Soviet counterparts. In the very beginning of this period and because of command channels, the treatment of "liberated" Austrians was much like that being given "defeated" Germans in Germany.[11] This soon changed.

U.S. OCCUPATION IN EUROPE

Although there had been practically no fighting in western Austria, in contrast to Soviet-dominated eastern Austria which was war ravaged in the extreme, United States forces still had had to deal with major relief and repair problems. Allied air strikes and last-minute German demolition had destroyed bridges and roads and rolling stock. The Nazi Administration had collapsed or disappeared. Schools and courts were closed, communications were immobilized, fuel and food were critically short. In addition, the area under American control had over one million refugees, most on the run from the Soviets. These refugees and displaced persons put an enormous burden on the military, as they had to be fed and sheltered along with the two million Austrians indigenous to the area.[12] It was an upside-down world which the tactical United States forces had to control and organize. Amazingly enough, this was accomplished rather quickly. Soon, civil government was functioning on local levels. On July 6, 1945, command over United States tactical forces in Austria was transferred from SHAEF to USFA. True, the status of Vienna remained to be settled, but the Americans were in Austria under their own command.

Vienna was a special case. All through the spring and early summer of 1945, wrangling between the Western Allies and the Soviets over zone boundaries and four-power control in Vienna continued. What the Western Allies wanted and what the Russians were reluctant to concede was surrender of the control of certain airfields in Vienna needed for the supply of Allied sectors in the city. Soviets were purposefully intransigent in order to buy time to consolidate their hold over Vienna's million and a half inhabitants, most of whom were still in a state of shock from the brutal actions of the Red Army.

A May cable from Truman to Churchill offered the following observation:

> I fear the Russians want to do things in Vienna which we would not approve, but I think they want equally much to do them in our name rather than carry the onus alone. Until we can have equal control, it seems desirable to maintain position that what is done there is done unilaterally.[13]

Finally, on July 4th and July 9th agreements were reached which offered a more or less satisfactory solution on zonal issues. It was another six weeks before the Western Allies could bring their headquarters to Vienna. The city was placed under quadripartite control on the first day of September, and the Allied Council held its first meeting on September 11th. The popular concept of four men in a jeep came into being.[14]

Initially, occupation authorities faced multiple humanitarian tasks:

getting war prisoners processed and returned home, sorting out and sheltering refugees and displaced persons, restoring law and order, and getting the economy back on its feet. Next came the tough problems of preparing for free elections, arranging for the disposal of the so-called German assets, and feeding the population. All of these proved to be be major headaches, the last two turning into what seemed, at times, perpetual headaches.

A Joint Chiefs of Staff memo of August 1944 had set down in broad and general terms some of the goals to be sought in Austria once peace came. Called for, were:

1. The prompt restoration of Austria as an independent state,
2. Furthering a sense of Austrian nationality and loyalty to democracy,
3. Long-range interest in the tranquility of the Danubian Basin.[15]

To the men on the spot in Austria a year later, this seemed terribly vague. In his book, *Calculated Risk*, General Mark Clark wrote:

> It seemed to me that when the discussion of territory was originally agreed upon in London prior to the ending of the war, our representatives were either ignorant of the Austrian situation or motivated by a desire to reduce our commitments and get our troops home. In other words, we had not known precisely what we wanted,[16]

And he added:

> The Russians knew exactly what they wanted: they wanted control of the Danube, the Zistersdorf oil fields, lower Austria and Burgenland as a bread-basket, and general control over airfields and communications networks.[17]

On the 1st of August 1945, General Mark Clark, as commander of United States Forces in Austria (USFA), received a directive from the JCS ordering him to serve as the United States member of the Allied Council and be responsible for military government in the zone assigned to the United States. The directive added:

> Any provisional government of Austria not recognized by all of the four governments, shall not be treated by you as possessing any authority. Only those individuals who recognize your supreme authority in your Zone will be utilized by you in your administration (clothed with supreme legislative, executive and judicial authority).[18]

The American forces in Austria learned rather quickly that the provisional government of Austria whose authority went unrecognized by the Western Allies was held in esteem by many Austrians. Indeed, with the exception of the British who remained sceptical, its most bitter critics such as Archduke Otto von Habsburg were outside the country.[19] Some second thinking seemed in order. Already in July 1945 the United States advisor for political affairs (Austria), John Erhardt, had signaled Washington that "to come to the question of the Renner Government, a prompt four-party agreement on an enlarged provisional government would be an invaluable help in administering Austrian affairs," and went on to say that "the only hope for a tolerable functioning of the Allied Commission with its four-headed divisions would be to call upon a provisional Austrian administration to submit proposals for legislative and executive action."[20]

On September 12, 1945, Chancellor Renner made an informal call on General Clark and urged that general elections be held not later than November while expressing his confidence that they would be free. Both men seemed to hit it off. Two weeks later, General Clark cabled the JCS urging the recognition of the Renner government, arguing that it "commands the general confidence and sympathy of the Austrian people to as great an extent as would any other non-elected group."[21]

Meanwhile on October 1st, the members of the Allied Council recommended to their respective governments that the authority of the provisional government of Austria should extend to the whole of Austria, subject to their guidance and control. Free elections were to be held not later than December. Following its acceptance in London, Paris, and Washington, this recommendation went into effect on the 20th.

The feelings seem to have been mutual. Austrian officials began to see, and use, the United States as a protector against Soviet encroachments. On October 27th, the Austrian Chancellor appealed to General Clark's chief civilian advisor for "disinterested" U.S. assistance to protect legitimate Austrian interests caught between Great Britain and the Soviet Union.[22]

The election of November 25, 1945 was the first free election in Austria in fifteen years. Only three parties were permitted to organize: the Communists, the Socialists, and the Austrian People's Party. Former Nazis were barred from voting. All three parties had roots going back into the First Republic, and the memories of the Civil War of 1934 between the Socialists and the Christian Socialists (forerunners of the People's Party) were still very much alive. On the other hand, there was an immediate need to put history aside and get an elected government and a parliament functioning. In spite of the fears of some Americans that the Soviet forces in eastern Austria might intimidate the voters into supporting the Communist candidates, little evidence has turned up that this was done.

ISSUES IN U.S. OCCUPATION OF AUSTRIA

Austrian voters had the opportunity of administering a resounding defeat to the Communists who wound up with scarcely 5 percent of the votes. The Austrian People's Party got 50 percent of the votes, and its leader, Leopold Figl, led a coalition government with the old archenemy, the Socialists, who polled 45 percent. In the *Nationalrat* (Parliament) the People's Party had 85 seats, the Socialists 76, and the Communists 4. Karl Renner was elected President. It was utter humiliation for the Soviet Union, the backers of the Austrian Communist Party.

What had happened? The Communists had obviously badly misjudged the general mood of the Austrian voters. They overlooked the continuing resentment engendered by the excesses of the conquering Red Army in eastern Austria and in Vienna. Many Austrians furthermore had served in Russia with the *Wehrmacht* and had seen the works of Communism firsthand. They wanted no repetition in Austria. Other reasons reduced the Communist role. Nominally 90 percent Catholic, postwar Austrians were generally either devoutly clerical, or socialists and anti-clerical. Neither side was tempted to vote Communist. The Communist insistence on disenfranchising all former Nazis was resented by many who felt it was the pot calling the kettle black. The Communist promises to "respect private property" were widely disbelieved. The Austrian Communists were for practical purposes out of the government. They would now have to subvert from without rather than from within.

The Austrians entered 1946 with a government of their own choice. True, the decisions of this government were subject to the review of the Allied Council where the single veto of one of the four occupying powers was enough to kill off the Austrian initiative. And true also, that many Austrians and Austrian leaders felt themselves serving time in a democratic "school of learning."[23] But, from the American viewpoint, the first mission of her presence, the creation of a democratic Austrian government, had been more or less achieved. Next would come the test of how well the Austrian government and the Allied Council could work in tandem. The biggest stumbling blocks were the issues of the German assets and the problems of food distribution to hungry Austrians in all the zones, issues which had begun to fray four-power harmony even before the New Year.

The German assets problem had its origin in the London Declaration of January 5, 1943 where among other things it was stated:

> ... the governments making this declaration reserve all their rights to declare invalid any transfer of or dealing with, property, rights and interests of any description whatsoever which are, or have been, situated in the territories

which have come under the control or occupation, direct or indirect, of the governments with which they are now at war or which belong or have belonged to persons, including juridical persons resident in such territories. This warning applies whether such transfers or dealings have taken the form of open looting or plunder, or transactions apparently legal in form, even when they purport to be voluntarily effected.

At the Potsdam Conference of July–August 1945, in what has been described as "a hectic and last-minute rush on the part of the British and the Americans to get the wrangling over and get home,"[24] the major powers got around to dealing with the issue of German assets in Austria. It had already been agreed that Soviet reparation claims would be met by removals from the Soviet zone of Germany and from appropriate external assets. What this meant for Austria was spelled out in Article IV, section 9.

> The Governments of the United Kingdom and the United States of America renounce their claims in respect of reparations to shares of German foreign assets in eastern Austria.[25]

Just what were German assets? It was not a question easy to answer. Following the Anschluss in 1938, the German government took over the economy of Austria. On occasion, duress was used to bring this about, but, in general, it was done in a manner to give at least the appearance of legality. For instance, the Austrian National Bank owned a share of practically every sector of Austria's economic structure. By declaring this bank to be German property, the Nazis got a controlling grip on the economic life of the country. From 1938 to 1945 capital additions were made. It was these additions, particularly the large oil fields in eastern Austria, which the Soviets now regarded as theirs. They argued that the Postdam Declaration had given these assets to them and that their ownership or control was properly a matter of their own concern and of no concern to either the Austrian government or the Western representatives on the Allied Council. It was a bold position. It was also a plan of action.

.   Almost as soon as the provisional government had received Soviet formal approval, the Russians were doing their best to bring into being a joint Austro-Russian oil combine. The pressure on the Renner government to sign such an agreement was almost irresistible. Much that was or would be valuable to a reconstituted Austrian economy had already been carried away, and the presence of the Red Army made any threat to carry away more very real indeed. The hope of the Austrian government had to be the Western Allies, particularly the United States.

In a message from the American Secretary of State to the United

States Ambassador in France (Caffery) the American position was summarized:

> Department's tentative views are that the creation of an economically self-supporting and independent Austria as per Moscow Declaration is consideration outweighing desirability of obtaining additional property for reparation pool. . . . For this reason Dept. holds in principle German property in Austria should remain as part of Austrian economy.[26]

On the same day in a message to the United States advisor for Austrian affairs (Erhardt), the Secretary of State outlined American interests on the issue of the German assets as follows:

> United States interest is: (a) to protect legitimate United States property interests; (b) to insure that Austria acquires equitable share of expanded oil properties; (c) to insure oil surplus to domestic Austrian needs.[27]

In general, the Western Allies took the position that the four occupying powers should collaborate in deciding what were and were not German assets, since all of them were officially dedicated to help the Austrians rebuild their shattered economy. This Western stand initiated a clear East-West faceoff.

In trying to explain their point of view to the Austrians, the Western Allies had the advantage of the credibility of their own free press. In many ways it offset the intimidating presence of the Red Army, and it proved effective in combating the untruths and distortions of the Soviet-dominated news services. The *Wiener Kurier*, put out by the Information Services Branch of the American Military Government, had a circulation of more than 250,000 (300,000 in 1947) the largest of any daily paper in Austria.[28] Written in German, it carried both world and Austrian news. In addition, the American Red-White-Red radio network with a listening audience of two and a half million, broadcasting from Linz and Salzburg, kept the Austrians informed and, in a sense, alerted.[29] The country itself was small enough so that what was heard in one part was quickly picked up elsewhere. The Soviets had their own controlled papers and also took to the air to impress upon Austrians how much they were doing for their benefit. But it was not much of a contest. The Americans were, by and large, believed. The Russians were not.

Beginning with the year 1946, the role of the Austrian government and the fate of the Austrian people were debated and fought out at two distinct levels. One was among the occupiers on the spot, the other, at the level of the Foreign Ministers. One, of course, influenced the other.

The year 1946 had hardly begun and the Austrian government had hardly organized and obtained recognition when it, together with the Allied Council, had to deal with a whole series of troublesome issues.

First, there was the basic problem of feeding the populace with the help of the UNRRA program and all the difficulties this involved, particularly in the Soviet zone. Then, there was the necessity of bringing about some sort of reduction in the occupation costs and an increase in agricultural and industrial production. There was also the nagging controversy about shipping rights on the Danube. All of these perplexities had to be viewed and treated against a background of slowly deteriorating East-West relations, globally and locally. Soviet vetoes were cast with increasing frequency.

A summation of that grim situation can be found in a message from the American political adviser (Erhardt) to the Secretary of State, dated February 26, 1946.[30] In it, Erhardt listed what he felt to be the three major goals of Soviet policy in Austria: (a) the maintenance of Soviet control over the Danube; (b) the insistence that the German assets in the Russian zone be regarded as Soviet property outside the jurisdiction of Austrian government or Council; and (c) that trade and/or commerce with the Soviet-occupied zone be solely under Soviet control. Erhardt added that, given the nature of these goals, "Austria had only the alternative of being a free and independent democracy or becoming a Russian satellite. . . ." He felt that unless some way could be found to reduce the size of the Russian military presence in the country and to stop Soviet penetration and exploitation of the economy, the chances of Austria remaining free were slim. He closed his cable with the warning that "time is working in favor of the Soviets."[31]

Much the same line was taken in a message brought to Washington by the Austrian special representative there (Ludwig von Kleinwaechter), who spoke of the constant Russian pressure upon the Austrian government to grant economic concessions or to yield economic rights. America would have to defend Austrian interests, for the Austrians could do little on their own.[32]

The question for America was how best to defend these interests and also the interests of the United States itself in the emerging tug-of-war between East and West. Two points seemed clear. First, the credibility of the Austrian government in the eyes of its own citizens had to be strengthened and Soviet-directed subversion against it contained. Second, the economic viability and independence of Austria had to be preserved.

By late winter of 1946, there was a united and strong feeling among the Western Allies that the Austrian government's power to "govern" should be enhanced and that occupation machinery should be reduced accordingly. Taking advantage of Article 14 of the original Control Agreement which offered an avenue to change, the British in February

1946 presented a draft of a new agreement. With but little change, it became the New Agreement of June 28, 1946. It brought about a smoother functioning relationship between the Allied Council and the Austrian government. Departmental staffs were made to correspond to their counterparts in the Austrian government. Zonal restrictions were lessened. Most important was a new provision (Article 6a) which stated that legislative matters submitted by the Austrian government, unless constitutional issues, would become operative 31 days after receipt at the Allied secretariat, unless there was unanimous disapproval of the four powers. The one fly in the ointment, at least as far as America was concerned, was a provision on which the Soviets had insisted which allowed the Austrian government to enter into bilateral agreements with any of the occupying powers. This, of course, permitted the Russians to preserve a substantial portion of the leverage they had exercised on the provisional government in the fall of 1945. But without this reservation, another Soviet veto in the Allied Council would have been inevitable.

Four days after the new agreement went into effect, the acting U.S. Secretary of State (Acheson) wrote to Secretary of State Byrnes in Paris outlining his reactions to it. He recommended leaving General Clark at his post as American High Commissioner and to initiate as soon as possible formal diplomatic relations with the Austrian government.[33] One sentence in this message carried considerable weight: "We consider it desirable for the American government to take the lead in securing maximum advantage for the Austrian State under this new Agreement."[34] This was, of course, a recommitment to the original mandate to keep Austria both free and independent. Austrian revisionists often quote it as an indication that the lines were being drawn for the coming Cold War and that Austria was to be integrated into the Western bloc.[35]

At the same time the Western Allies were working to broaden the powers of the Austrian government. The Americans were turning their attention to an eventual peace treaty with Austria. This inititative was prompted by several considerations. They included a desire to get all occupation forces out of the country and, indirectly, out of Hungary, since the Soviets justified their presence there with the need to supply and support the Red Army in Austria. They also involved the desire to relieve the Austrians of occupation costs, which were threatening to destroy their fragile economy. Also in mind was the coming retrocession to Italy of the South Tyrol and the need to offset this blow to Austrian pride with some good news.

The problem was that the Allies had never formally gone to war with Austria. The Austrians showed how to overcome this difficulty by pointing out that the Treaty of Saint Germain in 1919 had been considered a state not a peace treaty and urged repetition of this procedure. All American efforts came to naught, however, when the Russians refused to put it on the agenda in the April 1946 Foreign Ministers Conference in Paris and repeated this refusal before a second go-round in July. Another try would have to be made in February 1947 in Moscow.

One reason for Russian recalcitrance on the peace treaty issue was her continued tug-of-war with Austria over the German assets. Throughout the spring, the Soviets had been pressing the Austrians to negotiate the issue. The Renner government stalled for time, hoping that the new occupation agreement would offer some protection. But it was that very document which brought matters to a head. A little more than a week after it had come into being, the Russians expropriated all German property in their eastern zone, arguing that it was reparation due them under the Postdam rule. General Clark protested immediately. He agreed that the United States had never questioned the right of the Soviet Union to take over bona fide German assets in their zone, but he pointed out that just what constituted German assets had not been settled.[36]

The Austrian reaction to the Soviet position was one of bitter indignation. If the Russians could strip the country of its economic assets, then there was no practical chance that the nation could survive. A special session of the cabinet was called and an extraordinary session of parliament was set for the following day, July 11th. It legislated the nationalization of the bulk of the remaining properties claimed by the Soviets. The result was a strange dogmatic turnabout in which the Western Allies supported a state's right to nationalize the private sector while the Soviets affirmed its preservation. At stake was the interpretation under the new agreement as to what was and was not a constitutional issue. The Russians took the position that the new nationalization act changed the Austrian constitution and thus needed to be approved by all four powers. When the Western Allies failed to agree, the Russians simply refused to recognize the validity of the Austrian law in their zone.

In retrospect, the Soviet legal position on the constitutional aspects of the Austrian Nationalization Act was probably correct. Indeed, the American High Commissioner was advised by his own legal staff that the nationalization bill was probably invalid.[37] This opinion, of course, was not made public.

ISSUES IN U.S. OCCUPATION OF AUSTRIA

In an end-of-the-summer message from Erhardt to the Secretary of State, the observation was offered that the Soviets were beginning to feel that the new occupation agreement had "the tendency to let power in Austria slip from their hands."[38] He pointed out that the veto power in the Allied Council had been effectively transferred to the Americans, and it was now the Russians who were having their proposals knocked down. On Armistice Day 1946, General Clark made a speech in which he stated that the American people accepted as a trust the mission of helping Austria.[39] The speech was well received and thoroughly reported.

In the meantime, the food situation which had been reasonably good in the fall and winter of 1945–46 began to worsen in early spring of 1946. Until then, the United States and Great Britain had been able to maintain a ration scale based upon 1500 calories daily in their zones. The situation was leaner in the French zone and in the areas under Soviet control. The September 1945 agreement that all powers would share equally in meeting food demands in Vienna had been a failure from the beginning, with only the United States carrying through its obligations.

In a special message to the War Department in March 1946, General Clark drew attention to the serious situation in the Austrian capital where even the 1200 calorie limit was not being met.[40] He suggested that zonal rations be reduced and the resulting surplus be distributed in Vienna where the credibility of the Austrian government was visibly at stake, and where there was need to head off social and political unrest. Roughly one-fourth of the Austrian population lived there and was, of course, surrounded by the Soviet zone which, in turn, was the traditional bread-basket of the nation. But the Red Army, which continued substantially to live off the land, forbade the sending of foodstuffs from the Soviet zone to other areas of Austria and kept the amount coming into Vienna to a minimum. The announced intention of General Clark to maintain a 1200 calorie ration in the city and in the western areas put the Russians on the spot. However, it put the French and the British on the spot, too. Food was clearly becoming a major political weapon.

On the first day of April 1946, UNRRA took over the job of feeding the nation. The Austrian government was given the responsibility for the distribution of all foodstuffs in all zones. The ration basis was to be 1200 calories daily. The Russians did not hesitate to siphon off supplies sent in to their zone. The complaints of American military authorities went unheeded. General Clark let it be known that it was his belief that the job should be turned back to the military, but no positive action was taken on this. In August, it was announced that UNRRA operations would cease by the end of the current calendar year. After that date, other sources would have to be found. Indigenous sources would clearly be inadequate.[41]

The upshot was that by early autumn the food situation, particularly in Vienna, was approaching a critical stage. An October announcement that food rationing in Germany, the defeated enemy, would be raised to 1500 calories daily set off angry demonstrations in the capital and elsewhere. In the same month, the Russians tightened the food supply coming from their zone, though such action was contrary to the UNRRA agreement. The United States countered this action by promising quick delivery of foodstuffs from American sources. By mid-November, the government could broadcast that henceforth the daily ration would be 1500 calories in Austria as well. The Soviets demanded that the Austrian government be censured for taking such steps without prior approval from the Allied Council. There is no question that this development was a considerable blow to Soviet prestige. Soon thereafter, the Allied Council agreed upon a new food plan which granted unrestricted movement of foodstuffs throughout the whole of Austria. The agreement came two weeks before Christmas.

As 1946 drew to its close, the situation remained critical. The standard of nourishment in Austria was lower than that of any other West European nation. No substantial trade existed. The Austrians, who had hoped that the first full postwar year would produce a treaty and end to the occupation, were becoming resentful toward their occupiers. Most of this resentment was directed against the Russians who were seen as the major villains, but some bitterness was saved for the Western Allies and also for their own government.

Fritz Fellner, writing in Austria's *Zeitschrift für Aussenpolitik* has gleaned from recently declassified official American documents that the year 1947 placed Austrian survival on the agenda of history. These documents further show the extent to which Austria became part of those East-West tensions which were in the process of dividing Europe.[42] Again, as in 1946, this played itself out on the two levels of occupation policy and at Foreign Minister Conferences. Austria's importance in this struggle can be seen by the text of a message sent by the War Department to the American High Commissioner in Vienna.

> This government continues to regard Austria as of the greatest political and strategic interest. We cannot afford to let this key area fall under the exclusive influence of the Soviet Union, for if this should happen, it would not only consolidate Soviet domination of Danubian and Balkan areas but would also weaken our position in Italy, Germany and

ISSUES IN U.S. OCCUPATION OF AUSTRIA

Czechoslovakia. This government will therefore continue to support in every feasible way any government in Austria that preserves an independent or neutral orientation. There is accordingly no intention to withdraw our interest in Austria.[43]

This statement seconded a speech made earlier by General Clark assuring Austrians of the American presence until the Soviets could accept the Western position on the final disposal of the German assets.[44] It did not assuage the general's suspicion that there were forces in Washington prepared to "sell Austria down the Danube."[45]

In 1947 General George Marshall replaced James Byrnes as the American Secretary of State. Marshall asked Clark to accompany him to the Moscow Conference as his deputy. In his book, *Calculated Risk*, Clark writes that he was alarmed to find that General Marshall brought to Moscow no definite program on the Austrian Treaty.[46] To counter this, General Clark had his small staff prepare positions which he felt accurately represented what could and could not be conceded.

At Moscow, the sticking point remained the German assets. Here, the personal relationship General Clark had with General Marshall became a crucial factor. General Clark still feared that the State Department would engineer a compromise so crippling to the Austrian economy as to reduce the country to a Soviet satellite. He was determined to prevent such a retreat, and assuming that his suspicions had merit, he carried the day on this point.[47] Austria was not delivered over to the same fate which befell East Europeans. The proof of this would only become apparent later, however. The conference broke up without results.

There was disappointment in Austria that the occupation would continue. The Austrian Foreign Minister, Karl Gruber, in a bitter radio broadcast blamed the Allies for denying Austria its freedom.[48] The Americans, on the contrary, felt they had continued to preserve it. The man on the street in Austria was not quite sure what to believe. General Geoffrey Keyes replaced General Clark as the American High Commissioner. He had been Clark's deputy and knew Austria well. Like Clark, he was determined to fulfill the original mandate to keep Austria a free and democratic nation. Also, like Clark, he saw Soviet policy as a threat to this goal.

Austria's economy was strengthened substantially by several United States-initiated measures during the summer of 1947. In June, the Austrian government signaled Washington that it wanted to participate in the Marshall Plan. Austria was the only country in Europe to join the Marshall Plan while part of its territory was being occupied by the Red Army. It was a unique situation.

The Austrian economy got a supplementary boost in 1947 through the conclusion of three important agreements. Two of these agreements reduced occupation costs to the Austrians, and the third involved a major dollar relief program which enabled Austria to receive coal and food supplies. This guaranteed a decent nutritional balance for the rest of the year. America was making good on General Marshall's Moscow promise to Clark to get help to the Austrians. As might be expected, this help brought forth Soviet denunciations in the Russian-controlled press and in the Allied Council. Particularly galling to the Soviets was the Austrian government's willingness to accept American supervision of the distribution of relief supplies. The Americans countered that the Soviets were welcome to send along their own officials as observers. The Russians made no reply. Instead, they castigated the Austrian government, suggesting that such agreements were not in the spirit of the Moscow Declaration nor in conformity with the Control Agreement of June 1946. The Austrian government was warned that it would be held responsible for consequences resulting from its agreement to such conditions. But except for a continued press campaign against the perfidy of the government, nothing happened.

Also important to shoring up the Austrian economy was the introduction of a new wage-price policy enacted by the Austrian government in July 1947. This, too, generated critical comments in the Soviet-controlled press, but there was no Russian counteraction in the Allied Council. The economy improved.

In spite of its critical barrage leveled against the West through its controlled press, the Soviets did not initiate any major campaign of censorship of Western news media. One lone incident occurred in the city of Sankt Pölten (Soviet zone) where the French newspaper *Welt am Montag* was seized. The Russian High Commissioner immediately explained that it was caused by a misunderstanding on the local level, and he reaffirmed his determination to allow a free press. The next issue of the paper was distributed without incident.

Throughout the summer and into the fall of 1947, a special inter-Allied committee on the Austrian Treaty met in Vienna. The Western Allies remained firm on the position that a Soviet take-over of German assets could not be recognized. The Austrian Foreign Minister, Gruber, however, tried to pursue another approach in which some agreement would be sought with the Soviets against a promise of Soviet initiative on the treaty. This approach found sympathy among some members of the Austrian Parliament who feared that the well-known Communist Delegate, Ernst Fischer, was probably right when he decleared that "negotiations with the Russians could lead to a treaty but a refusal of Austrians to negotiate on the German assets would be proof to the Soviets that Austria was, indeed, a part of the Western economic bloc."[49] But the Western Allies remained adamant in their opposition to the so-called Gruber solution, and so did President Renner.

Shortly before the end of the year, Brigadier General Palmer of Keyes' staff was in Washington and made a report to the Joint Strategic Survey Committee of the Joint Chiefs of Staff. He had been sent by Keyes to urge further shipments of food and fuel.

Palmer stressed that, in spite of Soviet control over the eastern part of the country plus a large sector of the city of Vienna, the Communists had a hold on less than five percent of the population in terms of "true believers." The real danger to the security of Austria came from the potential intervention of the Red Army plus the hundreds of Russian agents operating in the western zones. He underscored the fragility of the Austrian economy and the need for America to pump goods and money into the country under an interim regimen preceding implementation of the Marshall Plan. He contrasted the small number of American combat troops to the large number of Red Army forces. All together, he painted a rather somber picture of Austria as the year 1947 closed out.[50]

By mid-January 1948, the Soviet Union produced its own proposal for settling the long simmering controversy over the German assets in Austria. Actually, the Soviet initiative countered a French suggestion introduced by General Paul Cherrière in October of 1947. The Cherrière Plan, as it was first known, suggested that all Soviet-claimed properties having anything to do with oil production, oil refinement, or oil distribution or exploration along with certain properties belonging to the *Danube Shipping Company* be transferred to Soviet ownership. This, he expected, would satisfy Soviet claims. All other claims would be settled by an Austrian lump sum payment or in trade to the Soviets. The Austrians would gain (or retain) control over all other properties currently claimed by the Soviet Union as German assets. The January 24 Russian plan accepted this program in principle, but insisted that the Soviets be free to take out profits in kind or in convertible currency (dollars) from the remaining property left under Austrian law. The Soviets also insisted that all disputes between them and the Austrians on the question of these assets be settled through bilateral negotiations. The Russians wanted a payment of 200 million dollars spread over a two-year period. On the basis of this proposal, new talks began in London in February 1948. At last, there seemed to be some hope that a treaty might be near.

The general Austrian reaction to all of this was optimistic. The Russian figures seemed exorbitant, and the Soviets would be taking a huge bite out of the Austrian economy, but there was the feeling that the figures could be scaled down somehow, and that the money could be found somewhere—probably in the United States.

The United States was shocked by being put on the defensive. The Soviets had come up with a seemingly workable solution to the hitherto insuperable German asset dilemma. The Austrians seemed to be wanting a treaty at almost any cost. It would be difficult not to go along. But did the United States really want a treaty? A memorandum from General Keyes back in November of 1947 had raised this question, and after giving careful analysis of the Austrian situation had concluded that a treaty which did not guarantee either the political sovereignty of Austria or its economic independence "would be worse than no Treaty at all."[51]

At this point the Communist putsch in Prague took place. It quickly became the issue of the day both in Europe and in America. It was the fire bell in the night that awoke the whole West. Sober rethinking was suddenly in order for both the Austrians and the Western Allies. The American Delegate to the London Conference on Austria, Samuel Reber, cabled Washington for instructions and posed the 64-dollar question: "Do we want a treaty under present conditions?"[52]

From Washington came the word that from a military point of view, any treaty which ended the occupation was undesirable. If, for reasons of economic or political motives, a quick multilateral settlement seemed imperative, then only with the clear provision that adequate Austrian security forces be recruited and trained prior to the American withdrawal.

A telegram from Erhardt to the Secretary of State, dated March 1, 1948, outlined the general effect the Czech crisis was having in Austria. A good deal of second thinking was going around. "While leaders of the non-Communist parties in the press are striving to give the impression that the Czech coup is not materially affecting the Austrian situation and that prompt conclusion of the Treaty remains a primary goal, a note of doubt and confusion is nevertheless apparent in private conversations at all levels."[53] In point of fact, the Austrians were having a good case of the jitters. The presence of the Western Allies seemed suddenly rather comforting.

In the meantime the London Conference had become hung up on the Austro-Yugoslav border problem. The resulting deadlock proved to be the handy excuse to suspend negotiations. The Western Allies and, indeed, the Austrians were off the hook, at least temporarily.

122

ISSUES IN U.S. OCCUPATION OF AUSTRIA

But at home there remained enough problems for the Austrians. Labor unrest, reinforced by general discontent over wage-price issues and by the continuation of a minimal food supply (1800 calories), led to noisy demonstrations and work stoppages. Local Communists were active in leading these outbursts and this, coming after the putsch in Prague, purveyed a grim sense of danger to the nation. There was some fear that it could spread into a skillfully prepared general political upheaval. The firm hand of the Socialist Trade Union leaders, however, prevented this. Unlike Czechoslovakia, where the Communist movement was strong, the weak Austrian party could do little without the assistance of the Red Army. But Erhardt, in another cable to Washington, still warned that continued supply of foodstuffs was vital to peace on the political front and that this supply would have to continue after the ending of the interim aid shipments.[54]

Now, events in Germany began to affect Austria. The beginning of what would become the Berlin Crisis was already apparent in April. There was fear that there would be a Soviet blockade of Vienna as well. The Russians were beginning to interfere with interzonal travel. By the end of June the crisis period in the blockade of Berlin turned attention to Vienna's equal vulnerability to any sort of Soviet blockade. The resulting isolation of the Austrian capital could certainly portend a Communist take-over in eastern Austria, although the U.S. legation in Vienna thought that a Czech-type crisis aimed at Austria's Sovietization was more in line with Soviet tactics in Austria.[55] In fact, nothing happened. The success of the United States and her Allies in air-lifting supplies into Berlin increased American prestige among Austrians. America was standing up to Russia.

Labor unrest again broke out in September 1948. The Austrian Communists organized a general strike for the purpose of disrupting the economy and embarrassing the government. It turned out to be a fizzle. Decisive again was the ability of the Socialist trade union leaders to keep their people in line. Planning for the arming and training of more men in the gendarmerie units went forward, as the Austrian government pressed the Western Allies on the need for security forces. A good deal of quiet help was forthcoming from the Americans and also the British. The new Austrian police later on furnished the cadre for the Austrian army permitted in the State Treaty of 1955.

In December of 1948 treaty talks resumed. And as the year closed out, the Austrian government had firm control over its own affairs and enjoyed widespread credibility with its own citizens. The economy had improved and in some sectors production was almost up to prewar levels.

U.S. OCCUPATION IN EUROPE

The food situation seemed well in hand, with a daily calorie ration exceeding 1800. Things were looking up.

The Americans could take pride in the fact that they had helped to give this nation a free government and the Austrian people a sense of nationality and purpose. The fight to create a truly sovereign Austrian nation was not yet won, but it was not lost either. The mandate had not been betrayed.

NOTES

1. J. Gannon, S. J., *The Cardinal Spellman Story* (Garden City: New York, 1962), pp. 222–23.
2. Gerald Stourzh, *Kleine Geschichte des Österreichischen Staatsvertrags* (Graz, 1975), p. 11.
3. Philip Mosley, *The Kremlin and World Politics* (New York, 1960), pp. 276–77; William Bader, *Austria Between East and West* (Stanford, 1966), p. 57.
4. Fritz Fellner, "Die aussenpolitische und völkerrechtliche Situation Österreichs 1938-Österreichs Wiederherstellung als Kriegsziel der Alliierten," in Erika Weinzierl-Fischer and Kurt Skalnik, eds., *Oesterreich-Die Zweite Republik*, 2 vols., (Graz, 1972), *1*, p. 66.
5. Gerald Stourzh, *Kleine Geschichte*, p. 13.
6. Text of the Declaration of the Soviet Government on Austria, *Austria: Red-White-Red Book* (Vienna, 1947), p. 201.
7. Department of State, *Foreign Relations of the United States 1945*, (Washington, 1955), *3*, p. 565, hereafter cited *FRUS*. Text also in Karl Renner, *Denkschrift* (Zurich, 1946).
8. Papers of Fleet Admiral W. D. Leahy, Box 5/8: Folder 24 (The Marshall Library, Lexington, Virginia).
9. Ibid.
10. Ibid.
11. Mark Clark, *Calculated Risk* (New York, 1950), p. 46.
12. Information Services Branch, USACA, Report of U.S. High Commission 1945–47 (Washington, D.C., Army Archives), p. 21.
13. *Leahy Papers*, Box 5/8: Folder 24.
14. The term "Four Men in a Jeep" was popularized in the media. It referred to the practice of mounted military patrols made up of military police from all four occupying powers.
15. Leahy Papers, Box 5/8, Folder 24.
16. Clark, *Calculated Risk*, p. 460.
17. Ibid.
18. Leahy Papers, Box 5/8, Folder 24.
19. Bader, *Austria Between East and West*, p. 29.
20. *FRUS 1945, 3*, 566.

21. Ibid., loc. cit., 1945, 610–13.
22. Ibid., loc. cit., 1945, 641–44.
23. Johann Luger, "Parlament und alliiertes Kontrollrecht 1945–1955," *Österreichische Zeitschrift für Politikwissenschaft*, 2, 1975, p. 229.
24. Bader, *Austria Between East and West*, p. 36.
25. Postdam Conference, II Doc. 1002. See also Harry S. Truman, *Years of Decision* (Garden City, New York, 1955), I, pp. 410–11.
26. *FRUS*, 1945, 3, 645–47.
27. Ibid.
28. See footnote 12.
29. Ibid.
30. *FRUS*, 1946, 5, 308–09.
31. Ibid.
32. Ibid., loc. cit., 1946, 508.
33. Ibid., loc. cit., 354–56.
34. Ibid.
35. See the following two articles in the March 1975 issue of the Austrian *Zeitschrift für Politikwissenschaft*: Rudolf Ardelt and Hanns Haas, "Westintegration Österreichs nach 1945," and Johann Luger, "Parlament und alliiertes Kontrollrecht 1945–1955."
36. *FRUS*, 1946, 5, 355–56.
37. Bader, *Austria Between East and West*, p. 73.
38. *FRUS*, 1946, 5, 363–64.
39. Ibid.
40. *FRUS*, 1946, 5, 354–55.
41. Ibid., loc. cit., 365–66, 371–72.
42. Fritz Fellner, "Teilung oder Neutralisierung" *Österreichische Zeitschrift für Aussenpolitik*, Heft 4, 1974, p. 206.
43. *FRUS*, 1947, 2, 1177.
44. Ibid.
45. Clark, *Calculated Risk*, p. 491.
46. Ibid.
47. Ibid.
48. Karl Gruber, *Between Liberation and Liberty* (New York, 1955), p. 113.
49. Gerald Stourzh, *Kleine Geschichte*, p. 22.
50. Palmer Report in Leahy Papers (Marshall Library, Lexington, Va.).
51. *FRUS*, 1948, 2, 1365–66.
52. Ibid.
53. Ibid., loc. cit., 1429–30.
54. Ibid.
55. Ibid.

7

Some Architects of
U.S. Occupation Policy Respond:
Summary of a Roundtable

Charles W. Sydnor, Jr.
Longwood College

The issues raised in the foregoing papers served as a major focus for Seminar Roundtable discussion. The open meeting brought together a number of distinguished public servants who had been instrumental in formulating and conducting policies that had guided the American occupation of Germany between 1945 and 1950. This essay will summarize the views expressed by these men during the Roundtable as they reacted to specific points in the seminar papers and responded to immediate questions from the audience.[1]

The Chairman of the Roundtable, Ambassador James W. Riddleberger,[2] took issue with *two* points Professor Jean Smith had made earlier in the day. First, he questioned Professor Smith's view that Secretary of State James Byrnes went out of his way to accommodate the Soviets. Ambassador Riddleberger argued that by proposing a forty-year treaty on German disarmament, what Byrnes had done was to attempt to assuage Russian fear of a German military revival. The Soviets rejected his offer. Moreover, Byrnes' Stuttgart speech of September 1946 calling for the formation of a German government advanced a policy that the Soviets did not favor.

Secondly, Ambassador Riddleberger found it hard to credit the notion that General Marshall promoted or hastened the onset of the Cold War. He reminded the audience that General Marshall had exhibited exemplary patience in dealing with the Russians during the Moscow and London Foreign Ministers Conferences in March and November 1947 and had tried his best to work out a solution to the problems in Europe with the Soviet Union within the framework of an agreement.[3]

One topic eliciting extensive exchange early in the Roundtable was American wartime planning for German occupation. In response to a comment from the audience questioning the extent to which advance preparations for the occupation were possible or advisable, Ambassador Riddleberger summarized ensuing events. Prior to the Moscow Conference of October 1943, President Roosevelt authorized Secretary of State Cordell Hull to agree to the principle of postwar occupation planning. Agreements reached at that conference led to the creation of the European Advisory Commission in London—the Anglo-Soviet-American body charged to work out policy details for Allied control of Germany after the war. According to Riddleberger, Roosevelt seemed hesitant to go beyond this step. The President was unwilling to make specific decisions about postwar occupation, in particular, and, as Secretary of War Henry L. Stimson's diary reveals, avoided decisions on postwar planning, in general. The President, Ambassador Riddleberger recalled, felt that no one knew what the Allies would find in Europe when the war ended, and he believed that the occupation would be a short-term matter. Both assumptions led Roosevelt to the conclusion that it was unwise to become tied to specific plans too early, and that provisional occupation arrangements could be worked out by army field commanders when the need arose.

Since the British and the Russians, by contrast, were advancing detailed proposals for German occupation, Ambassador Riddleberger concluded, the U.S. suffered a great disadvantage by not having precisely defined occupation plans until very late in the war. Even though the Allied agreement on zones was approved at the Quebec Conference of September 1944, the American occupation policy directive JCS 1067 and Allied agreement on the Control Council machinery did not materialize until after the German surrender.

Ambassador Robert D. Murphy[4] offered an assessment elaborating on the same point. Members of the European Advisory Commission assumed that the occupation would be brief and that their respective zones represented temporary divisions lasting only until a peace treaty was signed. Ambassador Murphy also recalled a conversation with President Roosevelt revealing the President's assumption that the United States would not be able to maintain its occupation forces in Germany for more than two years after the war. The President had advised Stalin of that projection. Two years represented Roosevelt's assessment of the maximum involvement the American public would tolerate once the fighting had ended. Ambassador Murphy indicated that he shared this view at the time.[5]

He also emphasized that Roosevelt's assessment unintentionally misled Stalin, and consequently, Stalin's Central Europe policies became based on the expectation of a brief American presence in Germany. Ambassador Murphy's observations, in turn, helped stimulate lengthy discussion of one of the most important topics raised in the Roundtable—the question of American-Soviet policy conflicts in Germany and the impact of that confrontation upon the evolution of the Cold War.

Mr. Paul H. Nitze[6] introduced the larger subject by observing that in 1945, the attitude toward the Soviet Union among those in Washington and those in Europe responsible for formulating U.S. policy was analogous to the view expressed by Walter Lippmann in his *U.S. Foreign Policy: Shield of the Republic*.[7] Mr. Nitze felt the majority looked upon the wartime Allied coalition as a necessary arrangement due to the threat Germany and Japan posed to the Soviet Union and the Western powers. In view of the profound differences between American and Soviet systems and objectives, many in Washington felt it unlikely that the U.S. and the USSR could remain peacetime allies. At the same time, Mr. Nitze continued, most of those responsible for U.S. policy felt that the United States had to try to maintain the relationship, since the consequences of a rupture between the U.S. and the Soviet Union were unacceptable.[8]

Mr. Nitze then added that a minority of dissenters existed who doubted the possibility of a successful continuation of wartime Soviet-American relationship and who argued that steps should be taken to deal with this contingency. Most prominent among this group, according to Mr. Nitze, were then Secretary of the Navy James V. Forrestal, Charles E. "Chip" Bohlen, who had served as Consul and First Secretary in the Moscow Embassy, and Ambassador W. Averell Harriman. Mr. Nitze also conceded that even among the majority who were more optimistic about the prospects for postwar Soviet-American cooperation, there was a general feeling that dealing with the Soviets after the war would involve real difficulties.

Once the war ended, Mr. Nitze continued, the hopeful view gradually changed as a result of the differences arising during negotiations with the Russians at Potsdam and at the Foreign Ministers Conferences in 1946 and 1947. As a result, by the spring of 1947, the earlier majority attitude about postwar relations with the Soviet Union had shrunk to a minority position. By mid-1947, most of those involved in implementing American foreign policy felt that the major objective of the United States should be to resist Soviet intentions in Europe.

To underscore Russian truculence in postwar negotiations over Germany, Mr. Nitze referred to an observation Governor Harriman[9] had made earlier. Governor Harriman had related that in a conversation with Stalin in October 1945 the Soviet dictator flatly declared that the Soviet Union had already decided to pursue an isolationist policy and would not continue the wartime relationship with the United States. Governor Harriman also remembered having been told essentially the same thing at that time by Maxim Litvinov, the man who had served as Stalin's first ambassador to the United States and had been Molotov's predecessor as Soviet foreign minister.[10]

Following Mr. Nitze's comments, Ambassador Murphy and Governor Harriman became engaged in a discussion over whether President Roosevelt's wartime policies vis-à-vis the Soviet Union and Eastern Europe had failed. Governor Harriman contended that they had not entirely failed, since Roosevelt's first objective had been to secure Soviet adherence to the United Nations. What had failed, Governor Harriman conceded, was the British policy—ironically, the very issue over which Great Britain went to war with Hitler—of preserving the independence of the Eastern European countries, Poland, in particular. Roosevelt had supported this policy, and in his dealings with the Russians, specifically at Yalta, he had secured Stalin's agreement to hold free and open elections in these countries. The resulting failure, Governor Harriman concluded, was due entirely to Stalin's unwillingness to keep agreements he had made with Roosevelt and Churchill.[11]

A later question from the audience about Stalin's intentions toward defeated Germany prompted Governor Harriman to return to this point and to elaborate on what he saw as major Soviet objectives in Europe in the immediate postwar period. Both Stalin and Vyacheslav Molotov, the Soviet foreign minister, had expressed to him their grave concern over the possibility of a rebirth of militarism in postwar Germany. Both Stalin and Molotov had lived through two German invasions of Russia and were therefore determined to keep post-Hitler Germany economically and militarily weak. Stalin, in particular, wanted to secure a share in the postwar control of the Ruhr industrial complex and therewith prevent German industrial capability from fomenting future wars. General Soviet policy toward postwar Germany was based on fear of German power and on respect for German industrial and organizational capacity—both recognized as superior to the Soviets'. It sought a Germany too weak to threaten the security of the Soviet Union ever again. This meant, as Governor

Harriman observed elsewhere, that the Soviet dictator opposed the reunification of postwar Germany under any circumstances. Stalin viewed even a Communist Germany as a dangerous rival who might replace the Soviet Union as the center of world Communism.[12]

Beyond the objective of keeping Germany weak, Governor Harriman claimed Stalin seemed intent upon exercising Soviet influence or domination over Western Europe. This he hoped to achieve not by invasion and conquest but through the Communist Parties of Italy and France. Stalin apparently believed that these parties would eventually become sufficiently strong to take over the governments of their countries, thus providing the USSR with dependable allies in Paris and Rome. Stalin's optimistic projections assumed an acute economic depression in postwar Europe which would create social and political chaos. It is in this connection that the plans developed by President Truman and General Marshall as Secretary of State for the economic recovery and reconstruction of postwar Europe became so critically important.[13]

Mr. Nitze and John J. McCloy[14] continued the discussion of Soviet policy in Europe with general comments supporting Governor Harriman's assessment. Roundtable members were then asked another question from the audience. Professor George K. Romoser of the University of New Hampshire, a seminar participant, wondered whether at some point in the immediate postwar period, the United States and the Soviet Union had reached a de facto or informal understanding with regard to respective spheres of influence in Europe. Professor Romoser also wondered whether, if such an agreement did exist, the arrangement produced a change in American occupation policy—namely, a U.S. acceptance of a divided Germany and recognition of Soviet domination in Eastern Europe.[15]

Governor Harriman responded first by saying that there were those in the postwar period who had suggested that the United States accept Eastern Europe as a Soviet sphere of influence. In his opinion, this view had been rejected, because it would only have encouraged a second Soviet thrust into Western Europe, and there never had been a formal or informal American recognition of Soviet domination of any part of the continent. Governor Harriman also added that as far as he knew, the matter of spheres of influence had not been discussed with Stalin by anyone acting on behalf of the United States. The division of Europe had developed with time and through unforeseen circumstances.[16]

Mr. McCloy agreed, remarking that he did not think the Soviet Union would ever have agreed to settle its postwar differences with the United States on the basis of mutually accepted spheres of influence. From his experience in dealing with the Soviets, Mr. McCloy said, their concept of negotiation was "what's mine is mine and what's yours is open season."[17] Governor Harriman interjected emphatic agreement, pointing to the remarks made by Soviet Communist Party Secretary Leonid Brezhnev during the May 1975 Moscow celebration of the thirtieth anniversary of VE Day. On that occasion, Mr. Brezhnev announced that the Soviet Union would continue to support liberation movements worldwide. This statement represented a repetition of a fundamental aspect of Soviet foreign policy— continuing assistance for Communist revolutionary and subversive movements everywhere. Both Governor Harriman and other Roundtable members did agree, however, that the Russians would make and honor individual agreements in particular situations, if they interpreted the circumstances to be in their favor—the specific case in point being Soviet approval of the boundary settlement and first moves toward normalized relations between the two Germanies.[18]

Ambassador Riddleberger applied these hypotheses to the other major occupation enterprise discussed at the conference. Ambassador Riddleberger analyzed at some length the crucial differences between the situation in Austria and the conditions in Germany and the corresponding significant difference in Soviet policy toward the former. Austria, he argued, had, in effect, been conquered by Germany and had been subjected to Nazi excesses to such a degree that when the war ended, the Austrian people had good reason to expect to be treated as a liberated area rather than as a conquered country.[19] From the standpoint of American policy in postwar Austria, this fact had been recognized and had conditioned the tone of the U.S. occupation there. As a result, the United States had underwritten the economic rehabilitation of Austria and never abandoned its pursuit of a peace treaty whose signing would remove all occupying forces.

Ambassador Riddleberger further observed that when the Austrian Treaty was finally signed in 1955 and the country thereby relieved of Soviet occupation, the Russians were prompted to accept and honor the agreement for two reasons. The first factor was Soviet Premier Nikita Khrushchev's coexistence policy which carried with it a Russian decision to cultivate better relations with Yugoslavia. The lack of an agreement on Austria had been a major obstacle in the path of improved Soviet-Yugoslav relations, since Russian failure to honor a pledge concerning Austria made Yugoslavs suspicious of Soviet motives in initiating overtures toward them. Secondly, the Russians may well have feared that if no Austrian treaty could be negotiated, the Western powers would attach their Austrian occupation zones to the Federal Republic of Germany and confront Communist Czechoslovakia with a military-geographic disadvantage roughly similar to what the Czechs faced after the German incorporation of Austria in March 1938.[20]

At a point midway into the Roundtable, Ambassador Ernest A. Gross[21] introduced a new dimension to the discussion. He observed that the question of applying the rule of law to a military occupation further complicated the evolution of U.S. policy. Normally, he continued, when a country defeats and occupies an enemy state, the occupier dominates and exploits the defeated. In this process the victor becomes a law unto himself. In the instance of the American occupation of Germany, this was not the case. Everything in the American political tradition had worked to prevent either the American military or the U.S. civilian occupation authorities from being given independent and unlimited control of the German civilian population. This was another reason why the United States needed some definition of its objectives before the war ended. This requirement, in turn, created the subsequent problems that arose in planning and running the occupation, since the development and implementation of American policy emerged from a tug-of-war among divergent points of view—a condition endemic to the process of policy-making in a democratic society.

The American occupation of Germany therefore represented an attempt to align its policies with American ideas and traditions. In the process, it built from the rubble and chaos of a shattered enemy state a representative society that could become a respected member of European and world communities. Ambassador Gross concluded that the fact that the Federal Republic of Germany has become a key member of the North Atlantic Treaty Organization and a member of the United Nations represents a triumph of American policy and its underlying rationale.[22]

Mr. McCloy responded that while he agreed with the logic of what Ambassador Gross said, he felt that in the case of Germany, President Roosevelt's insistence upon a policy of unconditional surrender during the war created a situation in which the surrender document asserted the absolute authority of the occupying powers and gave them unlimited power to impose their authority upon the defeated, irrespective of legal restraints. Ambassador Gross blamed this initial divergence from the precepts of the rule of law on President Roosevelt's unfortunate, misleading, and evidently spontaneous choice of words at the Casablanca Conference. If he had confined himself to demanding the "unconditional surrender of armed forces," it would have made a tremendous difference in the general understanding and acceptance of the concept.[23]

Ambassador Murphy added that he happened to be present at the Casablanca Conference, sitting right in front of President Roosevelt when the President used the words "unconditional surrender" for the first time. He understood at the time that Churchill had not heard the phrase before. President Roosevelt later admitted in Ambassador Murphy's presence that these words just came to him at the moment he uttered them.

Governor Harriman interrupted to disagree. He declared that there was, in fact, a discussion of unconditional surrender contained in the briefing papers assembled for President Roosevelt before the Casablanca Conference. Furthermore, Governor Harriman recalled, the matter of unconditional surrender had been discussed and agreed upon by the Joint Chiefs of Staff and had been accepted by the British Cabinet—although Churchill resented that it was an American decision developed without consultation with the British.[24]

Governor Harriman then went on to say that he had been opposed to the policy of unconditional surrender at the time and felt that the way in which President Roosevelt had announced it had been a mistake. President Roosevelt had himself later recognized that there were problems with respect to public understanding of what unconditional surrender meant. As a result, in the summer of 1944 Roosevelt proposed to Churchill that they publicly clarify the meaning of unconditional surrender so that there would be an understanding that the term was not an absolute demand for total servitude on the part of the German people once the war ended. Churchill, however, argued that the British had given unconditional surrender every consideration and did not want to change or explain it further. Governor Harriman concluded by saying that, in the end, he felt the policy of unconditional surrender had had no significant effect on the American occupation of Germany. The problems encountered in the occupation, he believed, grew out of the fact that there was no government in Germany and, initially at least, no way to form one.[25]

Another major subject which has already been discussed in preceding pages was the historic importance of the American occupation of Germany. A question from the floor, raised by Professor Richard Merritt of the University of Illinois, initiated a lengthy consideration of the utlimate significance of our prolonged presence. Professor Merritt asked participants to assess the most important long-run gain of the occupation. He also wondered whether the occupation policy goals of democratization and reorientation had in any way been altered, or perhaps even abandoned, as a result of the Cold War.

Ambassador Murphy recalled that the first object of American policy had been the search for one Allied policy dealing with Germany as a unit. We had failed in this, Ambassador Murphy felt, partly because the Russians began with the misconception that the United States would not maintain an occupation presence for more than two years. This had contributed to the development of difficulties in American-Soviet relations in Germany. Once the U.S. recognized the full extent of the difficulties and realized that, because of the Soviets, Central Europe could not be treated as a political and economic unit, American policy shifted in an effort to realize half the goal on the basis of a bizonal formula. The creation of a West German state through the combination of the American, British, and French occupation zones followed. The decision to abandon the policy of trying to attain American-Soviet agreement on Germany as a unit came after the Moscow Foreign Ministers Conference of March 1947, when Secretary of State George C. Marshall realized that no solution could be worked out in concert with the Russians. At that point, according to Ambassador Murphy, Secretary Marshall determined to pursue the bizonal policy—the amalgamation of the occupation zones of the Western powers into an economic and political unit.[26]

Governor Harriman then suggested that Mr. McCloy, the former U.S. High Commissioner for Germany, who observed the termination of foreign rule there, be called upon to offer his answer to the question. Mr. McCloy emphasized the importance of German economic recovery for Europe. At the beginning of the occupation, the whole economic and political structure of the country was in shambles. The American effort to initiate currency reform in the western zones was an important step toward recovery. The combination of currency reform, the initiative and industriousness of the Germans, and the subsequent influx of capital in the form of Marshall Plan aid resulted in the creation of a stable economy. This was essential for postwar economic recovery in the other European countries.

Equally important, Mr. McCloy continued, was the political miracle of postwar Germany. From the collapse and breakdown of the German governmental system in the spring of 1945, American policies helped create a stable, effective parliamentary system of government. Once the United States took the lead in permitting local elections in the face of criticism that this would lead to a resurgence of Nazism or neo-Nazism, the Germans chose public officials who were as good as or even better than their American counterparts. Moreover, German voters preferred men of moderate views; no radicals from the right or the left gained public confidence during the political reconstruction process.

In Mr. McCloy's opinion, this achievement was all the more remarkable, because both the men elected to office and the system under which they were elected were totally new. Few local officials or *Bundestag* deputies had sat in the *Reichstag* prior to 1933. However, a conspicuous number were included who had been members of the wartime anti-Nazi resistance. The construction of this stable elective system began at the local level, continued in the *Länder*, and ended at the federal or national level. The result was a political system whose health and durability remains in every respect as miraculous as German economic recovery. The restoration of economy and of polity, in conjunction, must be considered the permanent and most significant legacy of the American occupation.[27]

In addition, Mr. McCloy suggested there were two other areas in which American influence during the occupation had a salutary effect upon the development of postwar Germany. The first involved American initiative in helping to rebuild the university system in West Germany. The United States helped rejuvenate the Federal Republic's universities and the entire general education system, since these institutions of learning had been debased during the years of Nazi rule.

Secondly, after the military occupation had ended, the United States put pressure on the new West German government to effect a *rapprochement* with France. As U.S. high commissioner, Mr. McCloy had himself participated, recalling a visit Konrad Adenauer paid him shortly after he had been elected the first Chancellor of the new Federal Republic of Germany. During their conversation, Adenauer asked Mr. McCloy what he thought should be done first. Mr. McCloy called for an early Franco-German reconciliation. Specifically, Mr. McCloy told Adenauer that "we Americans are getting tired of coming over here every generation. You and the French stir up a war and before long it's a world war and we get involved in it. Now, you've got to cut that out." Mr. McCloy did concede, however, that Adenauer's subsequent successful efforts in behalf of Franco-German reconciliation were not entirely the result of his (Mr. McCloy's) admonition.[28]

Ambassador Jacob D. Beam[29] observed that one view of the postwar German situation is well-expressed in the popular French saying: "We like Germany so much we want two of them."[30] He wondered if the situation in Europe would be as stable as it is now if there were a united instead of a divided Germany. One reason the continent was experiencing stability, he suggested, was because Germany was not now united—a fact which Europeans and the Germans themselves have accepted for the time being. Mr. McCloy affirmed that it had been his wish that there could again be a united Germany that would represent the positive aspects of the West German experience. That hope was dashed because of the problems involved in postwar relations with the Soviet Union.[31]

Here, Governor Harriman interrupted to contend, rather forcefully, that in 1945 it was obvious to anyone who knew anything about the Russians, anyone who saw how they were treating the Germans and stripping Germany of all valuables, that the Soviets were going to impose a Communist system in their zone. Due to these circumstances, Governor

135

Harriman insisted, there was no possibility of "uniting a Communist Russian zone with a bizonia developing as the Germans wanted it with a Western type of civilization."[32]

At this point a query from the floor questioned the relationship of the Marshall Plan to the postwar situation in Germany. The questioner asked if General Marshall's frequently cited comments to the effect that the origins of the Marshall Plan could be traced to the Moscow Conference of March 1947 indicated that the Marshall Plan had been designed specifically to solve the German situation, since the agenda for the Moscow Conference had dealt almost exclusively with that problem. Mr. McCloy indicated his disagreement with the assumption that the Marshall Plan was intended purely to deal with the situations in Germany and Austria. General economic conditions in Europe in 1947 were such—the loans made previously to the British and the French were nearly exhausted —that further American assistance to Europe was absolutely necessary, or the United States would have faced the prospect of chaotic economic conditions in Britain and on the continent. It was Mr. McCloy's recollection that the Marshall Plan was initially designed to "assist the other European victims of Nazi Germany who found themselves in such desperate straits."[33]

Mr. McCloy then turned to Governor Harriman and asked him to elaborate on this point. Governor Harriman said that the question of economic assistance for Europe had been under study for some time before General Marshall made his proposals. Europe's problem in 1947 had not been confined to hunger; providing food would not have been enough. "There was no credit, there was no money to buy food, or raw materials to get the wheels of commerce going again." The situation was such that everyone thought Europe was going to collapse economically. The Marshall Plan was therefore not the result of a policy to save Europe from Communism; it was created to rescue Europe from the disastrous conditions that were the legacy of the war. Once the effort began, General Marshall and President Truman got the Marshall Plan through Congress with the help of Republican Senator Arthur Vandenberg of Michigan, the Chairman of the Senate Foreign Relations Committee. The entire plan was presented to Congress from the standpoint of saving Europe, and it received bipartisan support. The United States had an enormous interest in keeping the European countries as friends and allies. Germany and Austria subsequently were included in the Marshall Plan but were brought into the program as additions. The German and Austrian situations, Governor Harriman concluded, were not factors initiating the Marshall Plan.[34]

Mr. Nitze then continued that after Secretary Marshall made the speech at Harvard on June 5, 1947, outlining publicly for the first time the proposals for aid to Europe, the question of German and Austrian inclusion remained undecided. Throughout the summer of 1947, it remained a subject of persistent discussion among American diplomats in Europe. Mr. Nitze was sent to Paris to confer with all the U.S. ambassadors in Europe, and according to his recollection, "it was not decided until some months after Secretary Marshall's speech to include the whole waterfront."[35]

The relationship between the general European economic situation and the development of the Marshall Plan was the subject of a related point made by Mr. Jacques J. Reinstein[36] in the discussion following Professor Gimbel's paper. One extremely significant factor that entered into the preparations for the Marshall Plan and worked directly to accelerate the implementation of the aid program was the dismal picture presented by the American trade situation for the first quarter of 1947. At that time United States' exports to Europe for the year exceeded imports by ten billion dollars—an amount far in excess of the contemplated annual cost of any aid program. This staggering sum both underscored heavy European dependence upon the United States and graphically revealed Europe's incapacity to produce for herself. As a result, the problem of developing an aid program to make Europe self-sufficient appeared all the more urgent, a fact that worked directly to speed considerations leading to the creation of the Marshall Plan.[37]

The European scope of the Marshall Plan was also the center of a related discussion Governor Harriman and Mr. Nitze initiated in response to the paper by Professors Chotiner and Atwell. In that session, Governor Harriman pointed out that General Marshall had enlarged the European scope of his plan with an invitation to the Soviet Union and Eastern European countries, even though he strongly suspected that they would rebuff him. After all, the likelihood that the Russians would cooperate in a program involving the sharing of information was minimal. Governor Harriman and Mr. Nitze agreed that the portion of the Harvard speech containing the offer to the Russians had been drafted by Charles E. Bohlen, but Governor Harriman insisted that the invitation to the Soviets was General Marshall's own original contribution and that it was sincere. Not only did the Russians reject the offer, but they forced Poland and Czechoslovakia to withdraw from the program, after the governments of those two countries indicated an initial desire to be included.[38]

Governor Harriman stimulated another exchange relative to the Marshall Plan and the Soviet Union's response to it in the session following Professor Gimbel's paper. He raised the question of whether there was any relationship between the creation of the Marshall Plan and the Soviet

Union's activation of the Cominform (Communist Information Bureau), the agency through which the Soviets sought to coordinate and control activities of various Communist parties in all parts of the world after 1947. Governor Harriman suggested that the speed with which Moscow organized the Cominform after Molotov rejected the offer of Marshall Plan aid and walked out of the Paris Foreign Ministers Conference of July 1947 seems to indicate that the Soviets had been organizing the Cominform even before the announcement of the Marshall Plan. Otherwise, Governor Harriman noted, Molotov could have remained at the Paris Conference and delayed the Marshall Plan—a step the Soviets might have taken unless prepared ahead of time with plans of their own.

Professor Thomas T. Hammond of the University of Virginia responded to Governor Harriman's query by saying that the creation of the Cominform was probably the result of two things—the strain that then existed in Soviet-Yugoslav relations and Stalin's fears about the Marshall Plan's possible consequences. The latter, Professor Hammond observed, probably appeared to Stalin as a tremendous threat—a much greater danger than the Truman Doctrine, since Stalin had pretty well written off Greece at the time, and since the Marshall Plan raised the alarming prospect of enormous U.S. economic resources being brought to bear on the European situation. From Stalin's point of view, the obvious desire of many of the East European Communist leaders to accept Marshall Plan aid was even more alarming. As a result, Stalin apparently concluded that he had no other choice than to crack down and bring the countries of Eastern Europe under tighter Soviet control.[39]

What has been summarized here represents issues and views receiving preponderant emphasis during discussions and yielding key insights around which the seminar eventually revolved. If a single statement or a sole observation were to be made to best characterize a consensus among Roundtable participants—and doubtless the feeling among many others attending this extraordinary gathering—it would be Governor Harriman's observation that the United States' immediate postwar policies toward Europe represented one of the finest periods in American diplomacy and constituted achievements rarely surpassed in the history of this or any other country.[40]

NOTES

1. In preparing this summary of the Roundtable, I have used direct quotations sparingly. I have also attempted to convey the essence of the discussion as accurately as possible by organizing the chapter around the larger issues which emerged. As a result, the organization

of the chapter does not necessarily follow the sequence of the Roundtable, since the freely ranging discussion often touched on the same subject at widely separate points.

It should be emphasized that this chapter is not an analysis of nor a commentary on the merits of any of the views expressed by the participants. Accordingly, while I accept full responsibility for the accurate portrayal of what was said, I do not accept any responsibility for mistakes the participants may have made in their own comments. The complete text of remarks can be found in *Official Proceedings, The George C. Marshall Research Foundation, U.S. Occupation in Europe after World War II, Roundtable*—a transcript of the Roundtable made from audiotapes. Tapes and transcripts are deposited in the George C. Marshall Research Library in Lexington, Virginia.

I have also reviewed the Roundtable videotapes made by WCVE-TV of Richmond, Virginia, kindly made available to me for the preparation of this chapter. In addition, I have drawn on the transcripts of individual seminar sessions. They contain comments by Roundtable participants and by others relating to specific issues discussed separately in the Roundtable. Where relevant, I have incorporated comments from individual sessions.

Footnote references to Roundtable and session transcripts are hereinafter cited respectively as *Roundtable Transcript* and *Proceedings*.

2. Ambassador James W. Riddleberger spent more than half of his thirty-year career in the American Foreign Service in work related to German affairs. As Vice-Consul and then Consul in Geneva from 1930–36 and as Second Secretary of the U.S. Embassy in Berlin from 1937–41, he observed firsthand the development of events that led to the Second World War. During and immediately after the war, he served as First Secretary of the U.S. Embassy in London (1943–44) and as Chief of the Division of Central European Affairs in the Department of State (1944–47). Then, as Chief of the Political Section of the American Military Government in Germany (1947–50), as the Political Advisor to the Commander in Chief of the U.S. Forces in Germany (1949), and in the U.S. High Commission (1947–50), Ambassador Riddleberger was directly and deeply involved in the formulation and conduct of the policies that shaped the American occupation of Germany. Before retiring from the Foreign Service in 1968, Mr. Riddleberger served as the American Ambassador to Yugoslavia (1953–58), to Greece (1958–59), and to Austria (1962–67). (The biographical information for each of the Roundtable participants was assembled and provided by the staff of the George C. Marshall Research Library.)

3. *Roundtable Transcript*, pp. 1–5.

4. Ambassador Robert D. Murphy's diplomatic experience in Germany began in 1921 with his appointment as U.S. Vice-Consul in Munich— a post he held until 1925. After a decade in the U.S. Embassy in Paris (1930–40), Mr. Murphy was accredited to the Vichy government of Marshal Petain as Chargé d'Affaires. During 1941–42, Mr. Murphy served as President Roosevelt's personal envoy in French North Africa and directed the preparations for the Allied landings there in November 1942. Beginning in 1944 and continuing until 1949, Ambassador Murphy exerted a crucial influence on the development of U.S. occupation policy in Germany, first as the State Department's Political Advisor to the U.S. Military Governor in Germany, General Lucius D. Clay, and then as the Director of the Bureau of German and Austrian Affairs in the State Department. From 1949–52, he was U.S. Ambassador to Belgium, and in 1952 he served briefly as the American Ambassador to Japan before becoming Assistant Secretary of State for United Nations Affairs. Though he retired from the Foreign Service in 1959, Ambassador Murphy has remained an active public servant, most recently as a member of President Ford's Commission on Intelligence Activities.
5. Taken from the text of Ambassador Murphy's luncheon remarks of 23 April 1976, in *Proceedings*, p. iii, and similar remarks by Ambassador Murphy in the *Roundtable Transcript*, pp. 9–10.
6. The Honorable Paul H. Nitze served as Director of the U.S. Strategic Bombing Survey from 1944 to 1946 and as Deputy Director of the State Department's Office of International Trade Policy (1946) before becoming Director of the Policy Planning Staff of the State Department (1950–53). Mr. Nitze joined the Defense Department in 1961 as Assistant Secretary of Defense for International Security Affairs, and from 1963 to 1967 he was Secretary of the Navy. Before retiring from government service, Mr. Nitze served as Deputy Secretary of Defense (1967–69) and as a member of the U.S. delegation to the Strategic Arms Limitation Talks (1969–73).
7. Boston: Little, Brown & Co., 1943.
8. *Roundtable Transcript*, p. 12.
9. W. Averell Harriman served as the U.S. Ambassador to the Soviet Union (1943–46) and to Great Britain (1946). From 1946 to 1948 he was Secretary of Commerce in President Truman's Cabinet, and until 1950 he held the rank of Ambassador as the American representative in Paris to the European Recovery Program. Following his term as Governor of New York (1955–58), he served as Assistant Secretary of State for Far Eastern Affairs (1961–63) and as Under-Secretary of State for Political Affairs (1963–65). Among Roundtable participants, Governor Harriman held the distinction of having served as a close and influential foreign policy advisor to Presidents Roosevelt, Truman, Kennedy, Johnson, and Carter.

10. Ibid., p. 15. Governor Harriman recounted the incident of Stalin's remarks to him and the circumstances of the independent observations made by Litvinov during the general discussion following the paper by Professors Chotiner and Atwell. Governor Harriman's remarks are in *Proceedings*, pp. 100–01, 112.
11. *Roundtable Transcript*, pp. 15–16.
12. Ibid., pp. 47, 49. Governor Harriman's comments on Stalin's views on the question of German unity were made in response to Professor Gimbel's paper and are in *Proceedings*, p. 220.
13. *Roundtable Transcript*, p. 50.
14. The Honorable John J. McCloy was directly involved in both the formulation of American wartime policy and in the implementation of postwar objectives. As Assistant Secretary of War from 1941–45, Mr. McCloy worked on the development of plans for the postwar occupation of Germany. As President of the International Bank for Reconstruction and Development from 1947–49, he became thoroughly familiar with postwar Europe's economic problems. As U.S. Military Governor and High Commissioner for Germany from 1949–52, Mr. McCloy guided U.S. policy through the transition from military to civilian control over the occupation and oversaw the political transformation of the western zones into the Federal Republic of Germany.
15. *Roundtable Transcript*, pp. 54–59.
16. Ibid., p. 61.
17. Ibid., pp. 37–38, 60–61.
18. Ibid., pp. 60–61.
19. Ibid., pp. 5–6.
20. Ibid., pp. 7–8.
21. Ambassador Ernest A. Gross worked in the War Department from 1943–44 as Chief of the Economic Section of the Civil Affairs Division. In 1946 he moved to the State Department to become Deputy Assistant Secretary of State for Occupied Areas, a post that gave him direct responsibility for the development of policies for occupied Germany. After serving as Assistant Secretary of State (1948), Mr. Gross served as the U.S. representative to the United Nations Commission (1950–53) and as the American Ambassador to the Third, Fifth, and Sixth United Nations General Assembly sessions.
22. *Roundtable Transcript*, pp. 39–41.
23. Ibid., p. 42.
24. Ibid., pp. 43–44.
25. Ibid.
26. Ibid., pp. 10, 27. Governor Harriman offered a similar assessment of General Marshall's thinking. His comments came during the session following the paper by Professors Chotiner and Atwell and are in *Proceedings*, p. 110.

27. *Roundtable Transcript*, pp. 18–21.
28. Ibid., pp. 22–23.
29. Ambassador Jacob D. Beam's familiarity with German affairs dates from 1934, when he became Secretary of the American Embassy in Berlin—a post in which he remained until 1940. From 1941 to 1945, Mr. Beam was Secretary of the U.S. Embassy in London, and for two years immediately following the war served as a top-level political advisor to the U.S. forces in Germany. In 1947, he was recalled to Washington to become Chief of the Central European Division of the Department of State. In 1957 Ambassador Beam began a long period of critical diplomatic service in Eastern Europe. From 1957–61 he was the U.S. Ambassador to Poland, from 1966–69 Ambassador to Czechoslovakia, and from 1969–74 the American Ambassador to the Soviet Union.
30. *Roundtable Transcript*, p. 24.
31. Ibid., p. 25.
32. Ibid.
33. Ibid., pp. 28–29.
34. Ibid., pp. 29–30. In remarks made during the general discussion following Professor Gimbel's paper on Saturday morning, April 24, Governor Harriman returned to this theme. At that time, he emphasized the crucial role played by then Secretary of Agriculture Clifford Anderson in setting priorities for shipping American grain to Europe to feed hungry people rather than keeping it at home to fatten beef cattle. *Proceedings*, pp. 204–05.
35. *Roundtable Transcript*, p. 31.
36. The Honorable Jacques J. Reinstein spent some thirty years as an economist and economic advisor in the Department of State. During the Second World War, he worked as a State Department specialist for liberated areas. When the war ended, he became directly concerned with economic problems relative to the American occupation of Germany, and in 1949 became Chief of the Division of German Economic Affairs in the State Department. Mr. Reinstein also attended the Foreign Ministers Conferences of 1946 and 1947 and was a member of the State Department Policy Planning Staff at the time that body was engaged in intensive preparations for the initiation of the Marshall Plan.
37. *Proceedings*, pp. 208–09.
38. Ibid., pp. 110–11.
39. Ibid., pp. 207, 213–15.
40. *Roundtable Transcript*, p. 56.

8

Epilogue

Reflections of the U.S. Commanders in Austria and Germany

Fred L. Hadsel
George C. Marshall Research Foundation

The two principal American representatives in Austria and Germany, General Mark W. Clark and General Lucius D. Clay, were unable to attend the conference on United States Occupation in Europe, on which this volume is based. However, both men were subsequently interviewed at length.[1] Highlights of their reflections constitute the concluding chapter of this volume.

Austria

As the war in Europe drew to an end, General Mark W. Clark and his forces were completing their tasks in northern Italy. There was speculation that they might be going to the Pacific combat area, and when Clark was informed that he would be in command of American forces in Austria and United States Representative on the Allied Council, the assignment came "as a complete shock." "I had no idea where the troops were coming from . . . what arrangements had been made with the Russians . . . that I had to negotiate my entrance into Austria and get their permission to set up my headquarters in Vienna." Moreover, the line of authority to Washington was unclear, for General Eisenhower proposed that Austria be included under his command in northern Europe. While Clark told Eisenhower, an old and close friend, he would not interfere with this recommendation, "We have knotty problems to solve, and no two men are going to solve them the same way. I may solve one part of mine better than you solve (part of) yours. I would be against it." In the end, Eisenhower's proposal was not accepted, and Washington decided that Austria should be a distinct command. Clark soon became aware, however, that the decision did not resolve all his problems, since differences between his views of the Austrian problem and those of the Department of State continued throughout his two-year tour.

In August 1945, when Clark reached his headquarters at Salzburg in the American zone of Austria, he encountered delay and suspicion on the part of the Soviet authorities with respect to his entry into Vienna. The delay came, he knew, because the Russians wanted a free hand as long as possible in their eastern zone, which included Vienna, in order to seize property and consolidate their power. Soviet suspicion was displayed from the first informal meeting of the British, French, Soviet, and American representatives, well before the Allied Council met in Vienna. The Soviet Deputy General A. S. Zheltov immediately accused the three Western commanders of working together against the Soviet Union because of their wartime association in Italy. Clark made it clear to Zheltov that "If he wanted to start trouble so early in the game, it did not speak well for the future." As the Council began its work, it was evident that Zheltov was calling the shots. "We found that Zheltov was arrogant, mean, a double-crosser, whereas . . . Konev[2] wanted to be fairly friendly."

While the principal Allied Council opponents to United States policies were the Soviets, Clark did not find that his French and British colleagues always agreed with him. At the beginning, France was dependent upon the United States not only for its zone (which had been taken from the American territory) but for its food and other supplies. In reaction to this situation, the French representative, General Émile Béthouart, seemed on occasion to take positions primarily to demonstrate that the French "were not stool-pigeons of the Americans . . . I was never really sure that I could go into a meeting on a vital question like feeding (with their support)." However, Clark found that he could negotiate effectively with Béthouart, and because of many common interests, it

144

was possible to develop a good working relationship. The British representative, General Sir R. L. McCreery, "wasn't going to take anything for granted. He had his own opinions and he had a way of stating them." However, Clark could approach him "in any occasion and say, 'Your country disagrees, mine wants this' . . . and we could get together."

Early in the occupation, Clark clashed with the Soviets over two issues which showed both Soviet determination and, in his opinion, Washington's weakness. American troops had initially occupied, as agreed, territory in their zone north of the Danube and adjoining Czechoslovakia. The Soviets sought to obtain this portion of the American zone in order to control both sides of the Danube. In spite of Clark's protest, Washington ordered him to withdraw his troops, ". . . which was most disheartening for the Austrians."

A similar situation arose in connection with a large number of barges from the lower Danube, which the Germans had brought to upper Austria. The Soviets pressed for their return, but "we were particularly suspicious that they would be used to haul out dismantled results of their interpretation of reparations. . . ." They were also important as "the only bargaining point I had" in dealing with the Russians. On Clark's return to Washington for consultation early in his duty in Austria, he talked with President Truman about the situation. "I said that we recommend that we hold those barges until we could . . . get something worthwhile from them (the Soviets)." "And he said that as your Commander in Chief I give you instructions to do exactly that." Within two weeks, however, Clark received instructions from the State Department to turn the barges over to the Soviets. "I declined. I said the President . . . directed me differently. There was a lull of two weeks, and I got a message saying the President of the United States directs that you turn them over."

In the meantime, Clark faced a tremendous problem in feeding the local population. Not only had the Austrian economy been damaged as a result of the war, but the breadbasket for the entire country was in the eastern zone. The Soviets would not permit these resources to be used elsewhere in the country, and as a result, the Austrians were on a near-starvation diet. The American and British zones were able to open up a pipeline of supplies, based on their wartime movement up through Italy. Thus, they had the capability to provide some relief. In the autumn of 1945, Clark recalled, "After great thought, I proposed . . . (in the Allied Council) that we make the caloric rate fifteen hundred calories a day, which is starvation at that. The Russians just raised cain. Wouldn't approve of it and vetoed . . . I announced that regardless of their feeling I was going to raise it in the American zone to fifteen hundred calories, and I was going to give to the French sufficient food for them to do it." The Soviets had to agree, "Because elections were coming up and nothing could be worse than [the Austrians saying] we are starving in the Soviet zone."

The problem of feeding and housing the Austrians was greatly complicated by the existence of approximately a million displaced persons from Eastern Europe in Austria's western zones. For example, Clark found that he had no alternative but to use some of the former German camps to house displaced persons, since other Austrian facilities were so limited. This among other problems led to criticism in the United States of American occupation policy, which was reflected in identical letters from President Truman to both Clark and Eisenhower on the matter. Clark recalled that because of this, he and Eisenhower interrupted a long-planned tour of European battlefields in order to return to their headquarters to deal with the problem. Displaced persons, moreover, became an issue with the Soviet representative, who asserted that "[the Americans] were harboring many deserters which they [the Russians] were entitled to get back." Clark found, however, that the Soviet authorities exerted pressure to persuade persons to return, and when they succeeded they "disposed of them—our intelligence shows that they killed them." Therefore, he ended Soviet access to these camps, despite sharp criticism on the part of Russian authorities.

Initially, American authorities directly handled the food and supplies for Austrians and displaced persons, but in 1946, it was decided in Washington that UNRRA, directed by former Mayor LaGuardia, should control this activity. "My main issue with LaGuardia," Clark recalled, "was the way in which he was to distribute . . . the food, fertilizer, the plows . . . I said turn it over to me . . . I will give the Russian zone according to its population, but I'll see that it gets into the hands of the Austrian people . . . I couldn't convince my government to do that." It was turned over by UNRRA to the Russians, with the result that much of it was diverted from the Austrians for whom it was intended.

Political Turning Points

Despite Soviet economic advantages by virtue of their control over major Austrian agricultural areas, the principal industrial activities, including the Zisterdorf oil complex and the area around the capital of the country, Clark quickly perceived that the United States nevertheless had major political advantages. "We made it very plain that we came not as conquerors—we came as liberators." This was symbolically illustrated at the Salzburg Festival in 1945, when Clark unfurled the insignia for his troops, the olive branch and the colors of Austria. He repeatedly pointed out "that we had come in peace—with good will . . . to feed them, to help them open their schools, to do everything in the world to make life more . . . livable for them." "I had an educational program right down to every commander—personally to see to it that their men understood that they were to be courteous—polite—none of this arrogance . . . we were there to help."

American policy and practice—in sharp contrast to the actions of the Soviet forces—won strong sympathy and support from the Austrian people. This was clear very early in the occupation—notably in the attitude of the government led by President Karl Renner, Chancellor Leopold Figl, and Foreign Minister Karl Gruber. The Chancellor was a "spunky bulldog type," and Clark worked closely with him throughout his tour in Austria. "He was very friendly to the Americans, and I was very friendly with him." The Austrian government was constantly subject to Soviet pressure. Both the Chancellor and the Foreign Minister were in a most difficult position, being pressed from all sides, and General Clark, recognizing this dilemma, understood Austrian efforts to steer a neutral policy whenever possible.

The first dramatic demonstration of the direction in which the Austrian government sought to move occurred in November 1945, with the first elections. In retrospect, Clark recalled, "We were all scared of elections . . . because we were sure that the Russians would somehow manage to rig them . . . But I had gotten around a good bit, and I felt the warmth of the Austrian people for America . . . I still had misgivings, but I rather thought that there wouldn't be a big Communist vote." Even then "I was surprised that it turned out to be 5 percent . . . it absolutely flabbergasted the Communists." "From that time on, I was sure of the Austrian people . . . it caused us to double our efforts to demonstrate . . . our desire to reestablish them, as we had agreed, as an independent [country]."

Often it was possible to give only symbolic support to the Austrians—such as preventing the return of the famous Lippizzaner horses to Soviet control, displaying the Austrian crown jewels in Vienna (seized by the Germans but retrieved in the American zone), and being certain that the Austrian government, not the Russians, would have control of them. Clark believed then and three decades later that such actions were important, because they offered encouragement to a people facing desperate living conditions.

Another turning point in the continuing effort to reenforce the Austrian government occurred in the summer of 1946. The United States strongly supported revision of the Allied Council's procedure, which hitherto required unanimity to permit the Renner government to take any action. Under the new rule, unanimous Allied agreement was required to prevent action by the Austrian government. Hence, a single Soviet negative vote could no longer block the government. While this action did not lessen direct Soviet pressure, it did strengthen the capabilities of the Austrian government. "It meant that we could go into [the Council] with some assurance that we weren't going to be kicked around and [the Soviets] would say 'nyet.'"

Reparations and the Austrian Treaty

During the second year of Clark's tour of duty, the range of economic and political issues continued to be great, and their solution often elusive. For example, the need for a sound currency in Austria was imperative. The Soviets sought to exercise a role in currency issuance which would inevitably increase inflation, while the Austrian government, supported by Clark, succeeded in obtaining sufficient control to head off this danger. The Allied Council discussed at some length the size and nature of an internal defense force which Austria would clearly need in the future. Clark recalled that he advocated a force large enough and sufficiently armed to be effective, while the Soviets opposed his views.

But increasingly, as the Foreign Ministers of the four powers met during this period to deal with postwar Europe, the principal Austrian issue was that of reparations. "The Russians interpreted anything that was Austrian was German . . . so that they felt they had a right to dismantle factories, to take out anything they wanted, and they were shipping back to the Soviet Union all kinds of paraphernalia that was needed for the rehabilitation of Austria." Clark was adamantly opposed to the Soviets on this basic issue, because he believed that a compromise would mean the end of any possibility that Austria could be an independent nation.

At the same time, Clark found that the United States Department of State was inclined to accept the language on reparations which had been put into the treaties with Eastern European countries at the Paris Conference of 1946. Clark believed that this wording would "sell Austria down the river." It was ambiguous and would permit the Soviets to continue their confiscatory policy without restraint. When Clark was asked by Secretary of State Byrnes to be his deputy for Austria at the London Council of Foreign Ministers in the autumn of 1946, he at first demurred, in view of this difference with Washington. Clark finally agreed if he could bring his own staff in whom he had confidence and who, he believed, knew the facts. Despite initial acceptance of his position, he found in London that he had two staffs—one from the State Department and the one he had brought from Vienna.

There were, of course, many issues besides reparations to be decided before an Austrian Treaty was possible, although Clark believed that this was the critical question. When the Foreign Ministers Council reassembled in Moscow in March 1947, the difference between Clark and the State Department staff—now led by Mr. Benjamin Cohen and Mr. John Foster Dulles—remained unresolved. Clark was again reluctant to attend, but he did so at the request of the new Secretary of State, General George C. Marshall.

Clark found that the new Secretary of State had not been able to examine in detail the question of the Austrian Treaty, since he had assumed office only shortly before the conference. Despite opposition within the American delegation, Clark took on the responsibility of briefing General Marshall personally whenever the Austrian question came before the Council of Foreign Ministers. When the reparations issue finally came up for discussion, Clark told General Marshall that "this may well be the last day of the Council of Foreign Ministers . . . the (issue) is reparations and there is no possible solution to it." Clark recommended that the United States remain firm in its position. In the American staff meeting before the conference session, he discovered many delegates continued to support a compromise. It was a tense and long meeting, concluded only when General Marshall instructed Clark to draft the American position along the lines he had recommended. It was on this issue, Clark recalled, that the conference adjourned.

In reflecting three decades later on United States occupation of Austria, 1945–47, General Clark felt that there had been five persistent themes: the difficulty of dong business with the Soviets, the courage and willingness of the Austrians to suffer, the massive efforts of the Americans to feed the people and rehabilitate the country, the wisdom of supporting the government of Renner and Figl in every way possible, and the importance of standing firm on the question of reparations. Support for his policies on these matters had been less than complete on the part of the State Department, and the crucial decision by General Marshall on the Austrian reparations at Moscow had been a difficult but essential one.

U.S. OCCUPATION IN EUROPE

Germany

It is very easy, General Lucius D. Clay emphasized, to look back at the occupation of Germany from a span of some thirty years and forget certain basic elements of the situation in 1945. "You've got to remember that at the time we went into military government, we were moving into the acceptance of world leadership for the first time. After World War I, we had not only refused to go into the League of Nations, we had withdrawn from Europe . . . and become isolationists. When . . . by virtue of having won World War II, we were in a position of world leadership which we had to accept (but) which our people were not prepared for." While it was not analyzed at the time, we were "abandoning our old policy of living alone and accepting our responsibilities for world affairs."

The underlying problem was that the United States did not have a coherent policy to support its new leadership role. Policy had to evolve, and in the process conflicts were inevitable between broader and more isolationist elements within the State Department and the War Department. There were similar differences within the military, since it had not been accustomed to this kind of responsibility. And, of course, the press, sensing these divisions, likewise reflected opposing views. It seemed to authorities in the field that the press criticized whatever they did.

It was not surprising, therefore, that in 1945 there were divergent views concerning United States occupation policy. Not only was this reflected in the basic policy document, known as JCS 1067, with which Clay had no connection during the months it evolved in Washington, but a resulting combination of idealism and confusion manifested itself in various ways during the first year of German occupation. Two widely different illustrations will suffice on this point. Clay felt that some of the group being groomed to be the American component of the Control Council for Germany, "were really living in an imaginary world, . . . in which they were going to take over a German government in which there were ministries in existence." But it was obvious that "there were not going to be any ministries," and even if there had been, "under our rules of de-Nazification, there wouldn't be anybody to man them." He also found on a frustrating number of occasions that it was difficult to find the source of authority in Washington, because in the sharing of responsibilities between the War and State Departments, there were areas in which neither seemed willing or able to make a firm decision. Moreover, it was a situation in which "the administration of Germany could not be separated from the foreign policy action of the United States. So you were involved in a multiple show. And in a multiple show there is no boss . . . other than the President, and obviously you can't draw the President into everyday administrative problems."

First Year: Emergency Action

It was evident that the policy document designed to guide U.S. policy, JCS 1067, was unrealistic in some of its provisions, and General Clay's principal financial advisor, Lewis Douglas, resigned his position when he could not obtain modification of the directive's prohibition on economic rehabilitation. Yet, two very different factors so affected the implementation of this policy directive that it had a less inhibiting effect than might otherwise have been the case. In the first place, the document was secret, and it was well over a year before it became available to the public. Even though major parts of the directive being carried out appeared inconsistent, the press was not fully aware of the provisions for about a year, by which time there was an adjustment in the policies themselves.

In the second place, and more importantly, the German situation was so chaotic that it took five or six months before the military government realized some of the directive's difficulties. The situation was critical everywhere—the destruction of the cities, the lack of manpower (with the troops still in camps and forced labor having naturally stopped work), the desperate food situation, the standstill in production, the breakdown of transportation, and the influx of refugees from the East.

The economic problems were, of course, interacting. For example, the food shortage was critical, because the western part of Germany was traditionally dependent upon supplies from the eastern part of the country. These never became available from the Soviet occupation zone. And the immediate shortages in the cities were intensified by the breakdown of transportation between town and country. The initial relief supplies were large and of great help. However, during the second winter, there was a worldwide shortage. "We had a very low ration, and it was a bitter and cruel winter . . . but we were able to do better than we thought . . . we weathered it, and that was the worst of the food crisis."

In other realms, the coal required for fuel and production could not be produced, because the miners were starving and too weak to work. In industrial production, moreover, not only were wartime destruction and manpower shortages important, but the basic question of raw materials was a major problem. Raw materials could only be obtained through sale of goods. Yet, proceeds from such sales could be seized by foreign banks holding German debts. Hence, one of the many emergency actions was to obtain an agreement from the banks to allow the proceeds to be used to purchase raw materials and thus stimulate rehabilitation of the German economy. "So we had to get an agreement from the American banks that they would not bother this money. There were some seventeen banks that agreed they wouldn't seize any money that we got from German imports that we sold in this country."

Economic chaos was matched by government breakdown. By the end of the war, Berlin no longer controlled the country, and when the Nazis in the U.S. zone were dismissed, there was little if any authority left. While the tactical troops through their military government officers sought to revive the local government, ". . . there was no way to disseminate an order from the top to have it get down to the bottom . . . except through the military chain, and, of course, that was not built for that type of communication." It soon became clear that something more than just local government was needed, and "we set up the State of Hesse, which had not existed before. We had to combine (parts of) Wurttemberg and Baden . . . ," and then establish state governments in Bavaria and Bremen.

At the same time, "it was my decision that we have early elections . . . , that is, for the town and village, on the basis that the quicker we could get them back in the hands of the Germans, the better off they would be and better off we would be." It was interesting that the civilian professors of political science on Clay's staff had doubts about the Germans being ready for self-government, and it was "an army officer who was determined to have elections."

The evolution of local government proceeded with de-Nazification, a "formidable program," in part, because of the volume of records. Since the U.S. zone was the only one to undertake this policy systematically, it was especially difficult to be effective. A former Nazi could avoid de-Nazification by moving to another zone. "So this made it very difficult for our program to be as successful as we would have liked to have had it. However, I am still glad that we did it."

The international situation, of course, bore directly on both the economic and political problems of the first year. There were two matters of crucial importance. The Control Council of the four occupying powers was established in Berlin in the summer of 1945. "Unfortunately, it met and argued but never agreed." As a result, "there was never any progress made towards the establishment of a national government." Interestingly enough, in those early days, the Soviet representatives seemed to be willing to enter into arrangements to set up a central government, but they were always vetoed by the French. "I'm not sure that if the French hadn't the Russians wouldn't have."

The other problem was reparations. As Clay viewed the matter, if the Soviets removed plants necessary for Germany to survive without control or accounting, and the United States was at the same time contributing hundreds of millions of dollars worth of food to keep Germans alive, then "who was paying for the reparations? We were. And this didn't make sense to me . . . And so we stopped it, and it was never resumed. This was a major step forward really in bringing the German economy back."[3]

Second Year: Discouragement and Determination

By mid-1946, the various problems which had been dealt with on an emergency basis during the previous year were now being handled more systematically. Incentives were having their effect in coal production. The level of agricultural production was being increased. Local and state governments were in operation. Portions of the famous directive, JCS 1067, which could be implemented were being carried out, while those parts which could not be put into effect were either being modified or dropped. The long and complicated program of trying various categories of war criminals was well underway.

The same could not be said of relations among the zones of occupation, viewed as a whole. The French government, for example, was holding fast to its refusal to be bound by Yalta and Potsdam Agreements, since it had not attended the conferences. It maintained its stiff position on the Saar and on a number of other German issues. Cooperation with the Soviet government came to a standstill as disagreement on the reparations, as well as differences on other German issues, surfaced in the Allied Control Council in Berlin. The only occupation zones which cooperated with each other were the British and American. In part because the industrial core of the British zone complemented the more agrarian nature of the American zone, and in part because Clay found that his counterpart, General Sir Brian Robertson, came up with similar solutions to similar problems, there developed a whole range of cooperation between the two zones. By mid-1946, Clay was envisaging even closer arrangements, later known as Bizonia.

The international atmosphere contrasted with the progress being made in the American and British zones. The meetings of the four-power Council of Foreign Ministers during 1946 were stalemated on Germany. In the light of this situation, Clay believed that there was growing doubt in Europe whether the United States would remain committed to its policies on the continent. He therefore urged Secretary of State James Byrnes, whose delegation to the council meeting and peace conference in Paris in the summer and early fall of 1946 included both Senator Vandenberg and Senator Connally, to make a speech in Germany, "the important part of which was to announce our intention of remaining as long as anybody else did." "After all was said and done, even the Europeans doubted out intent . . . , even our allies, because we had pulled out so quickly after World War I."

"Mr. Byrnes finally decided to make the speech. He . . . visited me in Berlin first, and we went over it." Although he tried but could not reach the President directly on the principal point of remaining in Europe, he made sure that the President knew of his intention." The speech at Stuttgart, September 6, 1946 ". . . was a declaration of American policy that . . . was just as important in its time and place as the Marshall Plan was a little later." "You see, at the time of Stuttgart, the Communist threat was very real and particularly in Western Europe as a political threat. . . . The very fact that we were going to stay in Europe gave a great deal of courage to the non-Communists to begin to fight back politically."

Third Year: Germany and the Marshall Plan

If the highlight of 1946 had been the political commitment of the United States to see through its responsibilities in Germany, the most significant sequence of events of 1947 related to the Marshall Plan. At the time, the Germans "simply weren't making any progress towards economic recovery. And, of course, this was . . . a condition under which Communism thrives. In the lack of economic opportunity, freedom and all the other things that we value so highly don't mean very much. . . ." "With the Marshall Plan and the hope of economic recovery, we got political stability in Western Europe . . . And I think that it was the combination of American policy as expressed at Stuttgart and reaffirmed in a broader way with our help in the Marshall Plan that brought all this about."

The relationship between Germany (still occupied and divided) and the European Recovery Program was, naturally, extremely complex. Clay thought that there were at least three salient points worth stressing. First, a forerunner of some of the Marshall Plan methods had already been used in Germany, where food and supplies had been sold to the Germans for their currency, which, in turn, was used for a variety of purposes, including aid to the economy. "We were able to do many things with this money that helped to revive the German economy and to get it into (a better) condition. . . ." Second, there was initially considerable debate as to whether Germany would be allowed to take part in the Marshall Plan. "It was my contention, and I am sure that General Marshall accepted it, that if you left a vacuum in Western Germany, you would never get a recovery in Western Europe." "It was basic that the most productive country in Europe had to be brought back, if all of Europe was going to be brought back."

Finally, "By 1947, at the time of the enunciation of the Marshall Plan, it was quite obvious that the role of leadership in the free world had been accepted by the United States, and that, without it, there wouldn't be a free world, or at least one of the magnitude and size that we visualized and wanted to keep."

Of course, today this all looks self-evident and inevitable. But at the time, it was politically impossible for Germany to participate directly in the Marshall Plan. Instead, "We had to have the military government represent Germany. . . . We took very bright Germans right alongside us and listened to them with great interest, and within a few months . . . they had won their place. . . . It was a tremendously stimulating and interesting period . . . Western Europe . . . with great resources of people, of education, of intelligence . . . had just lost heart. And under the Marshall Plan you began to see competence show itself all over. There was an amazing resurgence in every respect. Although the economic one was the one that we were after, it was accompanied by political resurgence, cultural resurgence, and complete revival of the most democratic part of the world."

Fourth Year: The Berlin Blockade

While 1948 was a momentous year for Germany, with the enactment of the European Recovery Program, financial reform, and many political changes, the most dramatic event was the Berlin blockade by the Soviet Union, which officially began on June 24 and was not lifted for almost a year.

Clay had sensed a change in Soviet policy in the spring, and while he could not document the shift, he realized that it could be serious. When the actual stoppage of all land and water transportation from the western zones to Berlin took place, however, "I knew that it wasn't war. I knew immediately that it was an effort to drive us out of Berlin, on the theory, I think, that if we got out of Berlin, we would get out of Europe and that the political atmosphere would be such that Communism would thrive." Clay wanted to go in by land, for he believed "that if we had gone in on the ground, it would have broken the blockade without war." Our government was not ready to take that kind of risk. "We had demobilized, and we had very little military strength left at the time, other than a nuclear bomb." The government was only prepared to go in unarmed. "Well, this made no sense to me . . . And then, as an alternative, we started the airlift."

The technical difficulties, the superb direction, the remarkable efficiency of the Berlin airlift have been recorded in great detail elsewhere. There were, however, two major logistical problems which stood out in Clay's mind as he reflected on the blockade. The first was to mobilize all the available DC-3 (C-47) planes, even though they were becoming obsolete and could carry only three tons, in order to demonstrate that the United States and its allies could supply Berlin with the essential 4,000 tons a day to keep the city alive. A good start toward this goal was made during the summer, and with the smaller planes and some British bombers, the airlift reached a level of 700 or 800 tons a day. "But it was obvious this couldn't supply Berlin with coal and fuel [for the winter]. We had to have the large planes."

This led to the second problem, that of obtaining enough larger planes to sustain the airlift and achieve the minimal goal. Some of these planes (DC-4 or C54s) had begun to arrive in the summer, but the number wasn't sufficient. In October 1948, Clay went to Washington to plead for more large planes. The Air Force Chief of Staff, General Vandenberg's "contention was that if he gave us the rest of the DC-4s . . . he would be left without any (transport) planes." This was a sound military point of view. But "Mr. Robert Murphy (political advisor to Clay) and I were sunk, for without these planes we could not have . . . prevented the blockade from being successful." After the crucial meeting in the White House, however, President Truman said to the Secretary of the Army (Kenneth Royall) and Clay, "You are going to get your planes . . . And, of course, he was right, because it was a political decision . . ." not a military decision. "From then on, we had no trouble. And, as a matter of fact, on one of our big days I think we landed a little over . . . 12,000 tons in one day. Of course, today that would be child's play. But that was quite a performance in those days."

With all the crises and sacrifice of the blockade, it is extremely difficult to pick any single event which stands above the rest. However, "To me the most dramatic single moment was when Ernst Reuter, the Mayor of Berlin . . . came to my office and I said, 'Look, I'm ready to try an airlift. I can't guarantee it will work. I am sure that even at its best, people are going to be cold and people are going to be hungry. And if the people of West Berlin won't stand that, it will fail. And I don't want to go into this unless I have your assurance that the people will be heavily in approval.' And he said, 'General, don't doubt it for a moment.' And that is the way it worked out. They never weakened."

Final Year: A German Government

It was a complicated course of history from the local elections in the American zone during the first occupation year to the adoption of a constitution for the government of all of Western Germany in early May 1949, shortly before Clay completed his tour of duty.

The internal political scene was dominated by the development and rivalry of two principal parties, the CDU/CSU on the one hand, and the SPD on the other. The external scene was complicated not only by Soviet opposition to anything like a West German government, but also by the varying views of the three Allied occupation powers. When approval was given first by the American Secretary of State, General Marshall, and the British Foreign Minister, Ernest Bevin, and then by the French Foreign Minister, Robert Schuman, it was possible to move towards such a government by a constitutional convention in Germany. Of the many problems, "There were several disappointments to the Germans. . . . They thought that the restriction we put on with respect to the type and kind of industry they could have too severe, but, fundamentally, they were . . . unhappy about writing a constitution . . . leaving East Germany out, on the grounds that it would be their action that would have been interpreted as dividing Germany. They solved this problem by asking that it (be) called a Basic Law . . . and, of course, it had provision for any and all parts of Germany to become members thereof." From then on, the drafters of the Basic Law worked very hard and "wrote a very satisfactory constitution, under the principles we had laid down for some delegation of authority to the states." The final question that divided the Germans was the question of state support for parochial schools, with the CDU naturally favoring it and the SPD opposed. A satisfactory compromise was one of the last points to be worked out before its adoption by the Parliamentary Council on May 8, 1949, and its approval by the three military governors on May 12, just three days before Clay departed from Germany.

In this transitional period, the Germans were fortunate to have had the leadership of Dr. Konrad Adenauer, who ironically had earlier been relieved of his post as Mayor of Cologne on the grounds of his advanced age. "Ten years later, he was Chancellor of Germany and still going strong. . . . I said at the time that he was not only an able politician but that he had the competence and capacity to become a statesman, which he did."

In retrospect, Clay concluded: "Of course, to me, the most dramatic moment of my whole tenure in Germany was almost the last day I was there, when we approved the new Basic Law or constitution with the German Committee under the chairmanship of Adenauer. . . . I was very happy that this was done before I left Germany." The law "immediately went into effect and the elections were held early that fall, and the German Government has been in existence since."

Conclusion

Of the themes that dominate this period of the U.S. occupation of Germany after World War II—the emergence of a new, democratic government in Western Germany, and the evolution of American policy and leadership in the world—Clay concluded, in retrospect, there were two points worthy of special emphasis.

As far as Germany was concerned, the world may not have realized in 1949 how soon Germany would achieve full sovereignty, nor how well the Basic Law would serve Germany during the succeeding three decades. In addition to other circumstances affecting this development, "The Germans did well after the war in coming back because of one fact that they should be given credit for, they went to work. Not everybody did, but the Germans went to work, and one thing that is essential to recovery anywhere is a little hard work."

As to the significance of the occupation period in overall United States foreign policy, Clay looked at his task as one of bringing order to a destroyed Germany and of encouraging Germany in a new direction. "Fundamentally, we're an orderly people and an orderly nation, and gradually we bring order out of whatever chaos there is, as we did there, but it was not easy." But in a world sense, the United States was "obviously involved in abandoning our old policy of living alone, and of accepting our responsibilities for world affairs." This policy may have led to too much leadership. "We came to expect some countries to do what they didn't necessarily want to do." "We had set out to make them free and independent." "Now I think . . . we have accepted a role of world leadership which is based on coordination, cooperation, and persuasion, rather than the use of our power and force. I'm not sure we are entirely there yet, . . . but I think that we have come a long way. . . . If we are to get a free world that is to grow and to continue, it has got to be this kind of a free world, otherwise it isn't a free world. I think

EPILOGUE

that we have reached a maturity in foreign affairs that is a great credit
to our people. . . . After all is said and done, this has taken place in
a period of (less than) thirty years, and it's reversing the policy that was
in operation for 170 years . . . I think that it is a credit to our people
and its leadership. And certainly, in that initial period, this leadership
came from Byrnes, Marshall, and Acheson, and they were all working
for Truman."

NOTES

1. General Clay was interviewed 18 May 1976 by Albert Moffett, as
part of the preparation for an educational TV summary of U.S. Occupation in Germany, sponsored by the Marshall Foundation. General Clark was interviewed on 26 November 1976 by the writer
specifically for the Austrian portion of this chapter. Both transcripts
are in the possession of the George C. Marshall Research Foundation,
Lexington, Virginia. The page citation for the quotations were re-
tained in the working draft but dropped in the final version to assist
in the readability of the text.

    The point of view of this chapter should be made explicit. No
attempt has been made to recapitulate the full history of United
States occupation in Austria or Germany. This has been done in many
volumes, including published works and documents of the two
military governors themselves. Instead, this chapter contains views
of two U.S. representatives as they look back, after a span of three
decades, at this period of American policy in Europe.

    Consciously restricting himself to the material in these two inter-
views, the writer has sought to summarize the reflections of General
Clark and General Clay rather than to inject personal comments.
Therefore, statements in the chapter about Austria and Germany or
about policies and personalities are condensations of longer interview
passages. The quotations, of course, are taken directly from the texts.

    Both General Clark and General Clay have read their portions
of the epilogue. They have, however, left to the writer the task of
summarizing their conversations, which in total covered well over
one hundred pages of typescript. Hence, the task of providing a
reasonable reflection of the commentary has rested with the writer.
The responsibility for condensing these views, giving them an appropriate balance, and remaining faithful to the sense of the transcripts lies with the writer.
2. General F.M.I.S. Konev, Soviet Commander in Austria.
3. Except for a few plants already earmarked, General Clay stopped
plant removal from the U.S. zone by 2 May 1946.

159

CONTRIBUTORS

JOHN W. ATWELL, a graduate of Washington and Lee University, teaches at Hollins College. He did doctoral work at Princeton University in Russian history. Dr. Atwell is a frequent contributor to professional journals.

BARBARA A. CHOTINER taught at Hollins College, graduated from Wellesley College and just completed her doctorate at Columbia University. She held a Columbia University Presidential Fellowship during 1973–1974.

MILTON COLVIN, who holds a doctorate from Heidelberg and now teaches politics at Washington and Lee University, was formerly visiting Professor at the National War College and the University of Vienna. He was a member of the White House Commission on Refugees in Austria and Germany, 1948–1950.

JOHN GIMBEL of Humboldt State University has a doctorate in economics and political science from the University of Oregon. He was among the first contingent of Fulbright students to go to Germany after World War II. His books include *The American Occupation of Germany: Politics and the Military, 1945–1949* and *The Origins of the Marshall Plan.*

FRED L. HADSEL is presently Director, The George C. Marshall Research Foundation, has a doctorate in history from the University of Chicago, and was formerly U.S. Ambassador to Somalia and later Ghana.

HANS A. SCHMITT, Department of History at the University of Virginia, has written *The Path to European Union: From the Marshall Plan to the Common Market* and recently edited and completed the late John L. Snell's *The Democratic Movement in Germany, 1789–1914.*

JEAN EDWARD SMITH, who teaches political science at the University of Toronto, received his doctorate from Columbia University. He has been Visiting Scholar, Institute of War and Peace Studies, Columbia University; Fellow, Woodrow Wilson Center of Scholars, Smithsonian Institution; and Senior Research Associate, Center of International Studies, Princeton University. His publications include *The Papers*

160

of General Lucius D. Clay: Germany, 1945–1949, Germany Beyond the Wall and *The Defense of Berlin.*

CHARLES W. SYDNOR, JR., Department of History at Longwood College, is the author of *The SS Death's Head Division: Ideology and Personality in the Waffen SS, 1933–1945.*

EARL F. ZIEMKE of the University of Georgia did his doctoral work at the University of Wisconsin and was previously associated with the Center of Military History, U.S. Army. He is the author of *The U.S. Army in the Occupation of Germany, 1944–1946* and *The German Northern Theater of Operations, 1940–1945.*

OCCUPIED AREAS OF GERMANY

LEGEND:
- - - - LAENDER BOUNDARY

SCALE
0   20   40   60   80   100
KILOMETERS

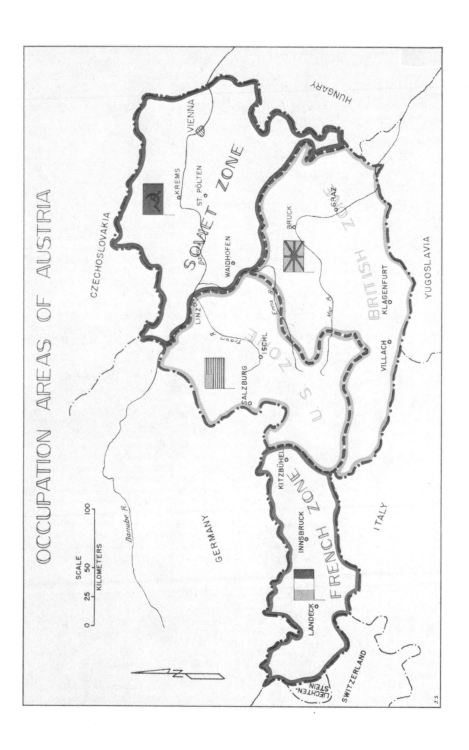

OCCUPATION AREAS OF AUSTRIA

SCALE
KILOMETERS
0   25   50   100

CZECHOSLOVAKIA

HUNGARY

VIENNA

KREMS
ST. PÖLTEN
SOVIET ZONE
WAIDHOFEN

GRAZ
BRUCK
BRITISH ZONE

LINZ
Traun R.
Enns R.
Mur R.
KLAGENFURT
VILLACH
YUGOSLAVIA

U.S. ZONE
ISCHL
SALZBURG

GERMANY

Danube R.

KITZBÜHEL
INNSBRUCK
FRENCH ZONE
LANDECK

LIECHTEN-STEIN

ITALY

SWITZERLAND

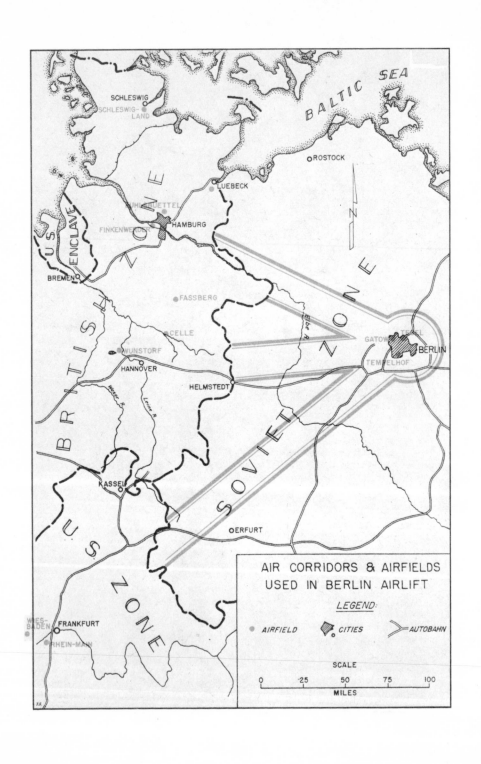

BALTIC SEA

SCHLESWIG
SCHLESWIG-
LAND

ROSTOCK

LUEBECK

BRITISH ZONE

U.S.
ENCLAVE

UHLENHUETTEL
FINKENWERDER
HAMBURG

BREMEN

FASSBERG

CELLE

WUNSTORF

HANNOVER

HELMSTEDT

Weser R.

Leine R.

Elbe R.

SOVIET ZONE

GATOW   TEGEL
BERLIN
TEMPELHOF

KASSEL

U. S. ZONE

ERFURT

WIES-
BADEN   FRANKFURT

RHEIN-MAIN

AIR CORRIDORS & AIRFIELDS
USED IN BERLIN AIRLIFT

LEGEND:

● AIRFIELD   ◫ CITIES   ⤙ AUTOBAHN

SCALE

0   25   50   75   100

MILES

Index

INDEX

and Pan-Germanism, 20
and provisional government, 106, 110, 112, 114–15, 148
and Socialism, 103, 107, 110–11, 123. *See also* Occupation zones; *Reichsrat*; Renner, Karl; Vienna
Austrian Nationalization Act, 116
Austrian People's Party (Socialist, formerly Christian Socialists), 107, 110–11
Austrian State Treaty (1955), 105, 119–20, 122–23, 131, 149

Basic Law, 41, 157–58
Battle of Kursk, 46
Beam, Jacob D., comments by, 135
Belgium, 89
Beria, L. P., 54
Berlin, 41, 57–58, 64–66, 68–71, 75–78, 90, 123, 152, 155–57; East Berlin, 64–66, 155; West Berlin, 64–66, 155
Berlin blockade, 60, 65–66, 76–78, 155–57
Bernstein, Barton, 86
Béthouart, Émile, 144–45
Bevin, Ernest, 92, 95–98, 157
Bidault, Georges, 91, 98
Bismarck, Otto von, 6–8, 9–11, 20
Bizonia, 38, 39–40, 89, 95–97, 134, 153
Blomberg, Werner von, 16–17
Bohlen, Charles E., 128, 137
Bolsheviks, 14
Borshchev, General, 53
Bradley, Omar, N., 75–77
Brezhnev, Leonid, 131
Brockdorff-Rantzau, Count Ulrich von, 15
Brown, Walter, 66, 73
Bundestag (German parliament), 134
Byrnes, James F., 38, 65–70, 72–74, 87–89, 91–95, 115, 119, 126, 148–49, 154, 159

Cabinet Committee on Germany (U.S.), 29–30
CAD (Civil Affairs Division), 28, 32
Caffery, Jefferson, 113
Casablanca Conference, 132–33
Catholicism, 8–9, 12, 17, 19, 111

CCAC (Combined Civil Affairs Committee), 28–29, 31, 33
CCS (Combined Chiefs of Staff), 28, 32–33
CDU (Christian Democrats), 56–58, 157
Chamberlain, S. J., 75, 76
Charter of 1814 (France), 5
Cherrière, Paul, 121
Cherrière Plan (1947), 121
Chotiner, Barbara Ann, 137
Christian Democrats. *See* CDU
Christian Socialists. *See* Austrian People's Party
Churchill, Sir Winston S., 30, 48, 87, 104, 107–08, 129, 133
Chuvikov, P., 48–49
Civil War of 1934 (Austria), 110
Clark, Mark, 107, 109–10, 115–17, 119–20, 143–49; as quoted, 143–49
Clay, Lucius D., 32, 34–35, 37, 41, 66, 68–77, 87–90, 93–94, 96, 143, 150–59; as quoted, 150–59
Clayton, William L., 97
Clifford, Clark, 72–73
Cohen, Benjamin V., 66, 94, 149
Cold War, 37, 42, 64, 65–67, 71–78, 86–98, 115, 118, 127–28, 133
and cold warriors, 86, 93
and detente, 77
and revisionists, 86, 87–89, 91, 93, 115
and traditionalists, 86, 87
Cominform (Communist Information Bureau), 138
Communism, 45, 60, 75, 78, 88, 94, 97, 111, 130, 136, 155; and anti-Communism (U.S.), 66, 78, 88, 94, 97, 136. *See also* Cold War; Communist Party
Communist Party, 17–18, 22, 45, 49, 50, 55, 72, 87, 96, 103, 111, 120–21, 131, 138
and Austrians, 103, 106–07, 110–11, 120–21, 123, 147
and Germans (KPD), 46, 50, 56–60, 87, 130
and Soviets, 40, 45, 47–48, 55–56, 58–60, 64, 75, 121–23, 130–32, 135–36, 138
and Yugoslavs, 49

INDEX

INDEX

INDEX

169

INDEX

INDEX